NEVER SKIP BRAIN DAY

Insights from a skipper

SANYAM SINGHI

NEVER SKIP BRAIN DAY
Insights from a skipper

First Edition 2025
ISBN: 978-93-343-9132-9

Imprint: Independently published.
Printed in India

Dedicated with love to my family, friends and fellow living beings with whom I share mutual existence and consciousness.

CONTENTS

INTRODUCTION

Throughout the span of human existence on earth, we have observed myriads of advancements in every sphere of life and nature around us. We, the homo sapiens, emerged in Africa around 300,000 years ago and from then till now, if we look at the development and modification our species went through, it will be just as awe-striking as the study about the Universe itself. It would have been simply impossible to stand at that point of time and imagine practically anything about what we are today i.e. 300,000 years after. The straight reason behind this is the human brain, which is arguably the most powerful living organ to exist in our world, , operating through the conscious mind, fails to perceive beyond what our five sense organs allow and even though it understands that there are things beyond what our senses can perceive, there are things which are yet to be discovered and observed, trying to argue about things like, 'What the human existence will look like around thousands of years from now?' or 'What sort of energy is controlling the Universe?' and all the other questions that are highly based on understanding of the power of possibilities that surround us, are often met by reasonings and logic based on what we already know combined with a very little acknowledgement of the unknown. We are conditioned to be oblivious to the unknown to the extent that if we try to think beyond what are known, giving much more value to the unknowns, going beyond the normal logic to the paradigm of impossibility, we would consider it as something abnormal. Yet we all somewhat still agree to the quote – "Anything is possible in the Universe". We cannot imagine an event that has never happened before because we have absolutely no available knowledge for our sense organs to even try sensing and picturizing them. For example- People in 1000 CE would have never imagined the existence of a device called mobile phone. Yes, they might have believed in the possibility of something like that, but to imagine the peculiarity of that thing would have been beyond their comprehension. All this being said- It's still the human brain at a particular point of time which had done wonders which the human brain at the period of time before that point could have never imagined.

This book deals with the psychology of mind connecting various phenomena through anecdotes, literature, science, history and general day to day life. It discusses how we give so much emphasis on the well-being of every part of our body but completely ignore the most potent and the most powerful organ- our brain. While some may argue that we are introduced to formal education right from our childhood, which is the brain acquiring meaningful knowledge and self-development, this book explicitly points out how feeding the logical mind with objective knowledge is not training the mind to operate at its full potential and how the greater and the most potent yet sensitive part of our mind, that is, the sub-conscious mind is left without any consideration.

In modern times, even though we have seen advancements in practically every field, mental health has been a tremendous issue to discuss. While we have reached to our neighboring planets, it's hard to comprehend why one of our neighbors who was doing well in every aspect of life, had an established career, planned retirement, social image and a caring family, suddenly wrote a note and hanged himself to death. In an attempt to address the issue of mental health, this book will strive to create a healthy self care and thought routine for your brain much like the routine people follow for other parts of their body in their weekly workout schedule giving each part of their body a special day to train. Meanwhile, the greater part of the brain, that is, the sub-conscious mind, which ultimately controls subtle nuances of every muscle group that people train in an attempt to remain physically fit, and the same brain which in a moment of displeasure can even inspire the person to finish his own body is left without any consideration. So, how important is a healthy thought and care routine for the brain is a no brainer. The Brain care routine won't comprise of any series of exercises but a mental series of perspective, thoughts and know how of the mechanism of life energy, field of infinite intelligence, the law of attraction and karma. The chapters will encompass training your sub-conscious mind and carrying the energy throughout every day and in every aspect of your life. It will inculcate a sense of harmony, wholeness and purpose in you such that you yourself will advocate – "Never Skip Brain Day".

1

"The present moment is filled with joy and happiness. If you are attentive, you will see it."

-Thich Nhat Hanh

MIND IN PRESENT

Have you ever wondered what would have happened if the apple had not fallen on Newton's head and lead him to discover the properties of gravity? The more intriguing thing to wonder about here is – What if when the apple fell on Newton's head, he was in deep thought about some stressful past event or anxious about foreseeable future. Such state of mind could have made him completely ignore the observation of apple falling on his head as some random natural event. It was his mind present in the moment completely detached from past and future open to observations and curiosity which did all the work. We need to accept that opportunities are abundant in present and that we just need to be observant enough to seize them. Saying this is, without any doubt, way simpler than actually being in the state of observation in the present moment after conditioning your brain and body for all these years to be always in a state of anxiety, worry, guilty, being cynical, questioning and judging.

Another example in this case is of Gregor John Mendel, an Austrian biologist. Born into a German farming family in Silesia, his young days went working in a garden. In the coming years of his life, this son of a struggling farmer went on to be regarded as the Father of Genetics and gave much insight about inheritance in his laws of inheritance. The question is simple, what inspired him to conduct experiments on a pea plant? It was his experience of working in the farm and those moments in which he was actually present in the moment while working which led him to observe curiously about how progenies are taking specific characteristic traits from the parent plants. It inspired him to go ahead in this field and conduct various experiments. Now let me ask you, what if that son of an impoverished farmer had spent all his days in wondering about how to make a fortune in future or how to secure higher rates for his produce, without observing things in the present moment and completely ignoring them as some regular natural phenomena. Some might say that it's natural to observe things if you are working on the same thing for years and truly it is, but the only thing I am trying to say is that behind every great discovery, there are that few moments where the discoverer was present in the moment delightfully observing things from the inside and outside. So, if few moments of great observations can lead to discoveries that had drastically changed the entire aspect of human existence and our way of living, imagine the impact of always being in a state of observation without judging the past, people and things or anticipating events in foreseeable future.

As I say this, am I referring to being emotionless? The answer is No; the point of focus is to monitor the cause and effects of our regular emotional states so as to get away from the vicious cycle of stressful emotions which serves as an impediment to us achieving a mystic observant state in the present moment. While all these age-old talks about being positive, thankful, cheerful, tranquil and grateful, to attract and live a happy and prosperous life seems very cliché and redundant, considering their acceptance in every school of spirituality, there has to be some science behind them. You must have heard the theory of impossibility of nothing and questioned its authenticity. While the logical mind may put forward multiple arguments against the statement, there have been various lores from all around the world about personalities in spiritual realm who had done wonders like living for a period much more than what we consider possible for a human to live. Although these lores, mostly belonging to medieval times, does not have any official authenticity, they are religiously agreed by the people of the region they belong to. I mean we should not even completely deny anything we cannot logically understand or perceive as it would make us of the same nature as that of the people who have earlier, denied the possibility of all those objects which we now use in our daily life.

Present Moment is revolutionary

Even our general conception of light is wrong scientifically. If I ask you randomly, what is light? The answer, most of the time, would be that it is that thing which enables us to see objects around us, wrong, the spectrum of light is way beyond our perception. It consists of invisible high frequency, short wavelengths- gamma rays, X-rays, Ultraviolet rays, invisible low frequency, long wavelengths- infrared rays, micro waves and radio waves and a small array of visible light that we perceive. Imagine how did some human discover these invisible frequencies of light which the normal human senses are unable to perceive? Much through the acceptance of the unknown, through observation of the present, curiosity that followed, experiments and constant reminder that at every point of time of our existence there had remained a thing yet to be discovered or observed and that science is not a fixed set of principles but an ever-evolving branch of knowledge. This simple example of light rays which we discussed has proved to be life changing. X-rays made advancements in the medical field, Ovens incorporated the use of micro waves for cooking, radio waves revolutionized the entire mass communication – mobile phones, radios, televisions and even airplane radars were made possible. Just the process of mindfulness observation-curiosity experiment leading to further and further of the same process brought about advancements and unimaginable revolutions in every sphere of life. Going forward, we can now agree that 'nothing has ever been impossible'. Also, I am not going against the laws of Newtonian science which is based on three laws of motion and overvaluing the element of possibility but I am taking a wholesome approach- there may be things which can go beyond the normal Newtonian science we know, maybe that many people who claimed about some supernatural events have observed those things but owing to their limited knowledge, failed to comprehend and elucidate those things or phenomena and maybe in future those things or phenomena gets unfolded by someone and become the general science of the time. The premise is that- things always exist before they are discovered- so yes- 'Nothing is impossible'

How present moment shapes the reality?

Let's come back to the main topic, that is, the present moment. Having explained the influence that the present moment had on our entire system, I will be going ahead further with how we can inculcate the habit of staying in present moment in our daily lives. For this let us first understand how our mind works, how we develop habits and how our entire thought process and behavior we exhibit forms a cyclic pattern. Understanding of all these is necessary as it is the concoction of past experiences, related thoughts, behaviors and emotions which inhibits our ability to stay in the present. Every day, we are exposed to countless experiences and thought. Suppose, we had a first-hand experience of a particular event, through our sense organs. It must have aroused some thoughts in our mind which is, biologically, the nerve cells in our brain forming a particular unique pattern corresponding to the experience to enable us to react to that experience. This unique neurological network sends an action potential electric impulse to the target part of the body with which the mind intends to react leading us to exhibit a particular physical behaviors or body language. Simultaneously, Chemicals are released in the body in the form of hormones and enzymes as per the influence of the experience and the whole process with all the electrical impulses, released chemicals and displayed behaviors creates an environment which makes us feel an emotion which again generates the same type of thoughts leading to a cyclic pattern. Biologically, for each particular experience of an event we had, the brain has assigned and created a unique neurological network which serves as the photographic memory of the event and each time we recall that experience or have a similar type of experience, the same network of neurons gets activated, the similar chemicals are discharged and we display a similar behavior and re-live the same scenario. The brain doesn't differentiate between the actual experience of the event and the recall or thought of the event because the neural network assigned to that experience is a memory captured by the brain and whether you experience that event again or just think about the influence of that event, the network circuit gets activated and the same cycle of thoughts, chemical discharge, behavior, environment and emotion is repeated. With the passage of time this repeated activation of neural circuits gets well established in the brain leading to a quicker future response to the experience it is related to, this is what we call an instinctive response. Body, also, gets addicted to the emotion and starts craving for the chemical reaction which causes it to feel that emotion. Eventually, the body becomes the mind and it makes us to think about the same event repeatedly, fire the same circuit of neurons to get the same chemical discharged and feel the same emotion, it is addicted to, again and again.

Having understood the science behind thoughts and reaction, now retrospect how do you feel while remembering a stressful past event or while predicting the foreseeable future based on past conditioning. Every time you think about them, you feel the same emotion and particularly after a heavy day, in spite of much resistance effort, you start to overthink while trying to sleep. This is because you have conditioned your body to be addicted to that particular emotional state to the extent that even when sometimes you have no reason to feel anxious, guilty, worried etc., you make up hypothetical stories in mind related to the experience and try to feel those overwhelming negative emotions again. In retrospect, I realized that feeling sad, worried or betrayed generates a wave of self-sympathy in us which creates a feel-good factor in our body that we did not deserve what had happened to us and consequently the body gets so much addicted to this feel-good factor that it desperately overestimates the quantum of negative things that has happened to us which we didn't deserve at all. As the saying goes, 'As a man thinketh in his heart, so is he', it is indeed your thoughts in the present which decides your future, thus, if you are continuously thinking about a dreadful past experience in the present moment, your body will get addicted to that emotion and will drive you to do anything to feel that emotion back again, making your future course of action aligned to the dominant thought in the present. Notice that unconditional love for self and others attracts love, feeling of betrayal attracts betrayal, feeling of lack attracts lack, feeling abundant attracts abundance – all of these examples of law of attraction is the outcome of the same mental thought process explained above. One mistake which people make while applying this law of mind, manifestation and attraction is that they try to feel abundant out of greed to attract abundance but when we talk about the science of manifestation, it is what we are constantly thinking in our mind is what we make our body get, physically and chemically, habituated and addicted to and this addiction is what subconsciously guides our future course of action. So, if greed is the driving force, anyone who affirms that he is abundant actually in his mind believes that he is not abundant and that he desires to be abundant in future. The dominant thought in present becomes that of not being abundant and thus in spite of all manifestation efforts they attract only misery. Remember the law of mind, thoughts and manifestation are the same thing. It is what you unconditionally believe in present that manifests and not what you desire with much anxiety. In spiritual realm, It is often emphasized that you can achieve anything if you are desireless, the same principle applies, if you are really desireless, in the present moment you will acknowledge that you have everything in abundance and that you are grateful, this feeling of abundance will generate a neural circuit in your mind and then chemicals and electric impulses will follow which after few repetitions will make the body addicted to itself and then the subconscious mind will guide your entire behavior and body language in such a way that you will automatically attract abundance. See an example of how our subconscious guides us to get the same thing which we think we always get - a person who constantly thinks that everyone is rude to him, establishes this feeling in himself and develops a subconscious which makes him behave rudely with everyone and then as he starts to behave in a rude manner with everyone, he again gets the same reciprocated. Thus, like attracts like. Therefore, when you are trying to manifest, stop desiring but start believing because desiring is based on a thought that you don't have a thing and 'don't have' attract 'don't have'. Believing has a power elucidated above clearly. Say every day to yourself - 'I am abundant', 'He/She loves me', 'I am that', and not 'I want to be abundant', 'I wish he/she loves me', 'I want to be that'. 'Fake it till you make it' is a tangible working principle given that you are actually faking a thing to inculcate the thing in yourself as truth and believable not just for the sake of it. Another famous much ignored line is,' a lie spoken multiple times, becomes a truth', this also holds true because we start to believe in a thing which we hear many times, and then our believe does the work. Believe, Become.

Empty your Mind?

'An idle mind is a devil's workshop' but still I want you to empty your mind in the present moment, detached from the past and the foreseeable future and to be completely present as an awareness in the moment. The saying 'an idle mind is a devil's workshop' highlights the same psychological concept I have explained earlier, a normal person who is sitting idle all day would normally wont practice meditation or mindfulness, he would rather be indulged in thinking something or the other related to past or foreseeable future and as negative thoughts generates self-sympathy (the feel good factor) most of his focus would be on the negative or stressful events, judging people, place or things around and thus all the destructive diabolical thoughts will get manifested in his future leading to destruction of the self and everything around him. Thus, the saying above actually corroborates the teaching of this chapter and is not a counter to this chapter. Contrary to the portrayal of the idle person above, when I speak about emptying the mind completely, the main focus is on getting detached from every thought of past, the people, the place and thinking that predicts the future based on the past. Sitting for a while, just as an awareness in a black quantum field remembering nothing. Achieving this present state in meditation and mastering this skill of being in present moment will help a person to get away with all the emotions which hinders its prosperity and enable it to get detached from anything easily. Mastery over self as it can be said. Once you are able to master this and gain complete autonomy over your thoughts, your body will stop becoming your mind and all the neural circuits related to negative emotions will breakdown over time. Now you can once again recreate your life as you can now use all your energy in feeding your fresh mind with elevated positive thoughts and emotions of bliss, joy, gratitude and make the body habituated to feel these constructive emotions and guide your subconscious behavior according to them leading to all the unknown events related to these emotions occurring unexpectedly in your life at some point of time in future. Such is the power of practicing the skill of mind in present.

To corroborate all what I have shared in this chapter, I don't need to give you any timeframe of tangible evidences. Just look within yourself and you must have experienced déjà vus, thinking something that has just happened, had already happened somewhere before, you must have fell into the trap of overthinking which, most of the time if not always, has been about negative experiences. In fact, the great minds of our generation, the minds behind the social media algorithm have designed its algorithm in the same way as our life is coded, you mention a topic or a product somewhere and then you get posts relating to the same topic or advertisements for the product across platforms. Contemplate all these with what you have learned in this chapter and it would make a lot of sense to you.

This chapter has not ended yet, while I have explained the science, the cause-effect relationship, the power of mind in present comprehensively, it is not as simple to control the mind, which is conditioned and programmed for negative and stressful emotions over the years, as it appears while reading. Most people complain about being disturbed by repeated thoughts and find it extremely difficult to empty the mind while meditating. They have actually developed anxiety towards thoughts while meditating. Meditation is not about thinking that you don't have to think. As a beginner, when you start meditating, you will be completely filled with thoughts and there is nothing adverse in it. Getting free from thoughts implies not paying attention to them. If they are coming, let them come. Don't go on to consider them as a disturbing element for your meditation as considering something as troublesome will only make you go deeper into thinking about the same. Remember mind in present is a skill which requires practice and meditation is a sort of mental exercise and like every other discipline you won't get mastery or extreme command over it in a day. Just like it took you years of constant conditioning to develop the habit of negative emotions, it will take you some time to undo them. So, here is how you should start with the meditation: -

- Sit in a comfortable posture, completely relaxing each part of your body.
- Close your eyes and take few deep breaths. Let each part of your body feel detached and relaxed.
- Now go deep into your mind, detached from everything, observe the blackness and try to hear the sound in your ears which all of us hear from within us in moments of silence.
- If there is a sudden gush of thoughts related to anything, acknowledge them. Don't think of them as disturbing and just let them flow, that means not attaching any importance or judgement to the thought. Realize for a moment that nothing matters and that you are practicing being in present. Come back to the blackness

of the present. It may happen that after few seconds of being in that blackness, you might encounter another thought. Just repeat the above process of acknowledging, remembering and letting go as nothing matters.

- It will happen that as a beginner, you will only be doing this process for some days. In the hindsight, you will realize that this process of thoughts coming and going was actually training your mind to develop a habit of letting go and overtime with constant practice, you will be able to completely be in that present moment, the black field of awareness, and be completely free of negative thinking.

2

"The virtue of justice consists in moderation, as regulated by wisdom."

-Aristotle

THE SUPREME COURT

The previous chapter discussed the significance of completely being in the present moment and how the brain captures a particular experience through creating and assigning a unique neural circuit which then signals the body to respond and create emotions chemically. The body with repeated experience of the related event, either in real world or in the world of thoughts and memory, gets addicted to the emotion, related chemical reactions and hormones. So, the higher the emotional impact of an event the higher the intensity of its mental and physical impact and then with repetition a belief system is formed and reality is manifested. This chapter will take a dig at how our logical mind, that is, the conscious part of our brain plays a role in this process and since our logical mind is always involved in judging external circumstances, analyzing situations to predict or decide future outcomes, it is the seat of the apex court of our body. All our judgements and interpretations, whether critical or uncritical, are based on the functioning of our logical mind. Thus, studying the nuances of our logical mind is of paramount importance.

Judicial system

A well-functioning, robust judicial system plays one of the most important roles in the development of any country by ensuring that laws are being properly implemented and also having an ethical check on the formulation of any law. An apex court of a country, not only interprets the law or provides justice but also have a say on the constitutional validity of any proposed law. When a judicial system of a country is efficient, it helps in the development of the country by keeping crime, corruption, civil issues and disorders in control. Thus, it brings efficiency in the operation of law and also enhances the economy as a country with a sound and efficient judicial system is considered business friendly. On the other hand, if the judicial system of the country becomes very rigid, inflexible, nonadaptive and inefficient, it will hinder progress of the country. Similar is the case with our body. Our body has got a judicial system in the form of nervous system and the apex court in the form of our conscious mind; the subconscious is the ruling constitution of our mind and body. If the operation of conscious mind is efficient, it will bring harmony and manifest miraculous reality while if its rigid and inefficient, it will manifest disharmony and destructive reality. The sad thing is the more logical our conscious mind is the more rigid and inefficient it becomes and still we are developing a society where logic is given paramount importance. I mean a basic logic is important for us to live but how

much logic, skepticism and analysis is too much as to not make our system rigid.
Hardly anyone thinks from this perspective. In the previous chapter as we understood that our thoughts shape our beliefs and then through a series of chemical and biological reactions, our body language and vibrations are altered and a reality is manifested based on our thought. Now, think, if everything we think and believe is based on our logical mind which is always engaged in pre-empting potential problems that may arise in the future based on its limited knowledge and past experiences and taking decisions to overcome them, the more logic we use, the more potential problems we will be able to find. For some it may sound good that we are able to find more and more potential problems and trying to prevent them because it will make our future comfortable but this is only half right, because in every moment of life, we are never physically present in the future and thus, if we consider finding more and more potential problems as a good attribute of our mind, we will end up with a life spent finding only problems and constraints. Since thoughts and believes create reality, a mind always filled with potential problems will manifest harsh reality because fear, anxiety and worry are the emotions associated with potential problems. Thus, higher the logic, miserable the man. Now, don't start referring great minds of our time to counter what I said in the lines above. Read about them and you will find that the greatest minds of our time had always valued intuition and intuitive knowledge above rationalism and logical

knowledge. You will read more about it in chapters to come. It is clear from above and in general observation of people around us that most of the people operate the apex court and the judicial system of their body in a very rigid (highly logical) manner. They forget that their logic is defined by what they already know while there is a vast ocean of knowledge yet unknown. There conscious mind (apex court) then passes decisions based on its logic and faulty external evidences collected by sense organs which causes the destruction of their own self by manifesting negative things in reality.

How to run the judicial system of the body efficiently?

Simply, by countering the logic and examining the validity of external evidences acquired by sense organs through interpreting the constitution, that is, the subconscious mind. Imagine you are going to have a meeting with a senior colleague with whom you have had bad experiences before. Your supreme court will alert you regarding the potential disagreements and arguments and chaos that might happen, it will try to make you ready by creating many potential scenarios in mind through its own analysis and imaginations. Your thoughts and beliefs will be full of what can go wrong, as a result, you will impart a negative body language and vibration during the actual meeting because all your reactions have been guided by the faulty decision-making system inbuilt in you. A negative body language will create arguments and disagreements and chaos and finally your earlier thoughts and believes will be manifested. At this point many people say that, - Oh I already knew that the person is very troublesome but hardly anyone realizes that it was due to their own extreme logic that a negative body language was created and their earlier thoughts manifested. The same situation could have been handled well if logic wasn't applied at the first place instead the case was handled with reference to the interpretation of the constitution, that is, the subconscious mind. Subconsciously, each of us know that people and their emotions are very subjective and that one who has been annoying earlier might not be annoying now, if we choose to not to see them through the lens we have already made for them. This was a prime example of how a rigid judicial system inside our body ran by high logic causes destruction of our growth by manifesting negative events while subconscious mind or the constitution is what is capable of preventing the destruction and promoting growth. In school days, while attempting a difficult mathematical problem, don't you remember that the more logic you have tried to apply, more complex and unsolvable the problem used to become while when you finally consult the teacher, the solution comes out to be rather simple. Similar is the case with everything in life, the use of logical mind should only be limited to the matters concerning our very survival, apart from them always go against your logical mind. Don't try to judge people because your conscious mind is faulty and rigid and often if you judge a person to be bad, he/she will turn out to be bad because it was your own manifestation of that person as explained in the example above. If you want to run a sound judicial system in your body, take every decision based on subconscious ethics and moral limit logical mind for extreme cases involving the question of survival.

What makes us so logical?

People consider being logical as a skill and often a thing to gloat about. The early years of most of us is spent in receiving formal education, which is aimed only at making the mind more analytical, logical and fit it with the basic expectations of the world. The basic flaw in the education system is that it is designed to train only a very small part of our mind, that is, the conscious or logical mind, while no focus is given on the larger subconscious mind. I have seen people who are very successful and people who have been a failure, but in most cases, both of them had got so many troubles. If academic success, career success, financial success etc. were the key determinants of happiness, then why there exist people who have had them all yet ended their lives in a miserable mental state. The reason being, the supreme court of mind, once trained to be rigid considers itself above everything, it works overtime without any fee and keeps on passing flawed decisions. It will throw the most successful person into thinking about ways to manage his current position, into an anxiety that something may take away all what he has achieved or it may create an ego that nothing can happen to a person if he relies on the decisions of his logical mind cum supreme court. Eventually a miserable mental state is achieved. The only difference between the actual apex court of the country and the court which our logical mind becomes is that in the actual court, the judge factually scrutinizes the evidences produced before it but the court of our mind accepts any external evidence which our senses perceive and believes it to be true. It believes whatever information is collected by the sense organs and applies some of the past information it already possesses and blindly delivers its flawed verdict which forms our opinion, reactions and believes. What makes us so logical is that we have been trained from the beginning to believe in what we sense. Since the beginning, our mental training is limited to logical mind.

How to take better decisions?

There is a saying that justice delayed is justice denied. Masses, after some major criminal event, often come out to protest and encourage the court to deliver a verdict as fast as possible. Their demand is reasonable but there may exist things related to the event which is out of their understanding, which has to be carefully examined and scrutinized by the court. Court runs on ethics, evidence and law and not just sheer public sentiment. I would say that if justice delayed is justice denied, what if a hurried judgement leads to a wrong decision and an innocent is put to severe punishment while the original perpetrator is set free, who will get to know? The sentiment of the masses will calm down and relax on the gravestone of buried justice.

In the case of self, people often hurry to take a decision because their natural instinct is that a delayed justice is a denied justice. They rely heavily on what is known to them(conscious) that they don't strive to know what is not known to them (subconscious). Eventually, most of the time the justice is buried and people create self-harming situations. I am not saying that never ever trust what your logical mind says but whenever you are going to take an important decision pause for some time, take a short nap, think afresh and then go for whatever your mind says. In this process, your conscious mind had consulted the subconscious constitution and examined the external evidence based on the system of subconscious ethics and justice. An intuitive hunch is felt and that is the wisest decision you can take at the moment.

Stop judging people

One of the key properties of the logical mind is that though it is yours, it is indifferent in passing judgements. It can judge others only to the extent you employ it to judge yourself. Now judging others doesn't only mean pointing out their shortcomings. Judgment is a neutral word to showcase assessing or analyzing someone's physical or mental trait. This feature is what leads to the buildup of insecurity in a person. Suppose you consider yourself very intelligent, this very fact will serve as a base when you judge others as to how much intelligent they are. It is okay till now but this mechanism can take very self-destructive form. There are things which are completely not in your control but if you have judged someone to be superior or inferior to you in terms of those things, it will always remind you of what you lack even if the thing which you lack is irrelevant. It will eat you up and build an absolutely unnecessary inferiority complex. All of these operates through thinking and since thinking is what creates believes and reality, a destructive reality is manifested. That's why in spiritual realm; it is highly advocated to not to judge others (but who cares). The demonstration of this effect is much present around us. The orthodox uncles or aunts, who always gossip about or condemn or interfere in the lives of others for not being attached to culture, who condemn or ridicule or mock their friends when their friend's son or daughter do something which is culturally not supported like inter caste love marriage etc. Often, their very own children do the very same thing against which those uncles were advocating and ridiculing others all their lives. Why? Because when you judge or mock or ridicule others for a thing, you build an inherent fear that such thing should not happen in your own case and since fear is an emotion and emotion drives thoughts and believes, eventually believes driven by those fear gets manifested into that reality. Thus, never judge others.

On an ending note, I would say that learn to give long holidays to the supreme court of your body and rely more on your constitution (subconscious mind). If relying on subconscious is also not bringing any positive results, it means that the subconscious is also filled with accumulated unwanted and involuntary remnants of conscious thinking. In this case what we do is – A constitutional amendment, and just like a constitutional amendment is a detailed and hefty process in reality. In the same way, clearing subconscious mind of maladies needs time. The easiest way is to shut down the supreme court (conscious mind) and keep thinking as much positive as you can. Go to the extent that people call you mad for not reacting to their provocation. Don't react and with time subconscious correction will automatically happen.

3

"Everything we call real is made of things that cannot be regarded as real."

-Niels Bohr

IS REALITY AN ILLUSION?

In spiritual context, you might have often heard that reality is nothing but an illusion. You might have also heard that you are not you- the person you know yourself to be, but you are the soul, the consciousness which interconnects everyone and everything. All these lines of wisdom might have baffled you or you might have just considered them esoteric words of spiritual world which is of no use to you. The main purpose of this chapter is to breakdown reality and discuss the nature of reality in a context much easier for a person, who is not very connected to the spiritual world, to understand. Also, before we go ahead let me clarify one thing, spirituality doesn't mean just praying to God or believing in God, it is much more about knowing how the spirit (soul/aatma) actually works in a way that can be scientifically justified, practicing those principles and striving to attain singularity, after all God is referred to as '*Param-aatma*' (supreme-soul) and you are an '*aatma*' (part of the supreme soul), so how exactly you can connect to that supreme soul which you are part of is what actually spirituality deals with. It is not just about feeling positive and praying and believing. Let's now start with chapter and dive into the realm of unknown and build an understanding of it brick by brick.

Perception

The word perception means the way something is understood, interpreted, assessed and to perceive things in our external environment we make use of our sense organs. Through eyes we see, through ears we hear, through tongue we taste, through nose we smell and through skin we feel and then the sum total reality is formed and interpreted in the logical part of the brain. For example, when you are stuck in a traffic jam, through your eyes you are seeing all the vehicles stuck, their colour, model, and other attributes, through your ears you can hear the honking and other sounds of engine etc., through your nose you can smell the irritable polluted air of the city, through your skin you can feel the weather. Finally, your brain forms the complete picture. This is what a person in the materialist realm calls reality. This is what you and me have until now called reality. Someone spoke bad about so you start disliking that person, because in reality you have heard that person speaking ill about you. Someone appreciated you and you felt good; it becomes a part of your reality. The point is how you felt that your experience is bad or good, was it bad because the person said ill about you or was it because you interpreted it in such a way?, I know it sounds a bit idealistic and that if someone speaks bad about you, it can be interpreted only as bad but the point is that interpreting things is what is in our control and if interpretation creates reality why not interpret things as the way we want our reality and not the way our logical brain is saying that it is actually happening, The foregoing lines might sound very irrelevant in day to day context of life because we have been taught to react according to the environment, punish those who harm us and embrace those who care for us. There is a famous line by Mahatma Gandhi "An eye for an eye makes the whole world blind" and often this quote is ridiculed by super intellectual masses. I don't want to discuss the life of Mahatma Gandhi or debate upon his ideas. I have few questions for the logical, rational, super intellectual revolutionary people who talk about fighting for their rights, fighting for wrong, fighting for the nation (by the way I am referring to human civilization as whole), seeking revenge, seeking pride, glory. First, how do you know that what you are fighting for is real and not something interpreted by your brain as such? and when does the cycle of fight and revenge, pride and glory end? who will ultimately win and who will be alive to see who won? History bear evidence that the greatest of all the empires in the world have fallen and yet infinite lives have been lost in fighting for those empires. The only sane argument is that if we become idealistic and stop fighting others would take advantage and attack our nation and culture and destroy it. So, it is basically the insecurity, lack of trust, division and lust for power is what have created revolutions and wars. And where does this insecurity, lack of trust, believe and faith comes from? it's from our perception of reality through our sense organs and use of our super logical mind. I must add that history proves that the worst of the men have been those who were highly educated, logical, rational, practical. Example- Osama bin Laden, Adolf Hitler etc. You may say that there were good men too who were highly educated and rational, true, but at times people have to take decision for the greater good of humanity and not for the goals they are associated with and it requires not being very logical at times because some goals can be very destructive. Logic always suppresses and kills the magic.

Logic always kills the magic

Our brain has two aspects, subconscious which is intuitive and conscious which is logical and rational. We spend our entire academic life sharpening the logical part of our brain and that's why I say that the education system is flawed. In materialistic life we live, we are taught to solve problems, are trained in analytical skills from childhood. The thing these people don't understand is that the logical brain not only solves problem but it is way smarter as it tries to find and create potential problems and tries to solve them beforehand. A sharp logical mind uses information we already have to predict future problems and finds ways to prevent those problems. This skill is developed in humans since ancient times because at that time humans had to constantly think about protecting themselves from surrounding danger of wild and thus our mind became not only a problem-solving machine but also a problem finding machine, a problem creating machine. We sense a thing; we interpret it according to the information we already have and create reality full of problems.

Let's go deeper, I said "Logic always kills the magic". Let's break it down with the story of the invention of airplanes. In 1880s, there published articles in newspapers in the United States that scientists have found that a human flying machine is only theoretically possible and that the size, weight and proportion which would enable a machine for human to fly according to principle of physics would be such that it would be impossible to create physically. Everyone accepted this scientific knowledge of the time and considered it as logical. Who were adamant in believing that a human flying machine can still be made?, WRIGHT BROTHERS, Now see how logic kills the magic, the idea of that time that a human flying machine is not practically possible was so ingrained in the minds of common people that those who even saw Wright brothers testing Airplanes between 1905-1908, refused to believe it and they interpreted that they are seeing some other object flying in the sky, a blimp, a hot air balloon etc. It was after extensive public events demonstrating the airplane that people actually believed in airplane, years after it was first tested. Such is the nature of reality and the logical mind which perceives the reality.

Heinrich Hertz discovered radio waves - the life line of all modern telecommunication. These radio waves cannot be seen from eyes, cannot be touched and felt, cannot be heard, cannot be smelled or tasted. So basically, a human cannot experience this radio waves logically, then how was it discovered by a human? through observation, through experimentation and through a believe that there exist things which can't be perceived by human. Our super intellectual friends have always questioned the existence of soul and God, to them I ask, what if God and soul are of the nature of a highly energetic frequency (which indeed they are) which just like those radio waves cannot be perceived or seen, touch, heard or felt tangibly by humans but simply observed. Second question to those who say that we will believe in God only when scientist discover Him, you have read above that how all the great findings, inventions and discoveries happened when the discoverer first believed in the idea and not the logic, so how can you find God if you don't first believe in Him? To find something that you don't know you need to explore the unknown whereas logic only allows you to explore what you already know. It is non-sensical to think that you can find or discover a new or unfound thing with the knowledge you already have without striving to know more. People who have embraced spirituality have observed the presence of God just like Heinrich Hertz observed radio waves. Still, you cannot see radio waves you can already experience its functioning; in a similar manner you cannot see God you can experience his function once you forget your logical constraints and dive into spiritual realm. I said 'Logic always kills the magic' and here it is concluded, with logic you can solve or create or correct what already is found, with intuition or subconscious or infinite knowledge you can explore what is yet to be found, that is what is magical, and that is what the so-called modern education system is not teaching.

Sense Organs are imperfect

You have studied how we create reality in our minds by perceiving objects in our external environment through sense organs. The intellectual mass always quote science in everything. A mere reading of Human Sense Organs chapter in Class 7 biology book says, Human eyes can only see light in a frequency range of 430-770 THz (terahertz), Human ear can hear frequency of sound between 20-20000Hz, skin receptors can detect vibrations between 10-50 Hz in case of flutter, light touch and up to 250-350 Hz in case of deep vibration and pressure. Similar limitations are there in our sense of smell and taste. Dogs have a better sense of smell than humans. Cats and dogs have a better sense of sight in terms of distance and night vision than human. What does all of this mean? that there are things which exists but humans cannot perceive them at all.

If I wave an orange handkerchief and ask you if this is orange in colour, true or false? You would say true. But the same colour orange doesn't exist for a dog because dogs have dichromatic vision. There may exist creatures who can perceive much more colours than humans. Basically, it depends on the wavelength and frequency of the particular light ray and how much capable the eyes are to form a perception of colour. Humans see orange, when a light wavelength of 590-

620 nm or light frequency of 484-508 THz strikes the eye. The same wavelength and frequency may form a different colour in some other creature's eye. So how can any subjective thing be universally true or false. Sense organ's capabilities are always subjective. Crazy thing is for you until now reality is what you touch, see, hear, taste, smell or feel.

In Indian philosophies, be it Jainism, Buddhism, Hinduism, the various spiritual schools, the core motive is always to control the sense organs. In the earlier chapter you have read how what you believe gets manifested into reality, but here is the twist until now you were only believing through your sense organs which are scientifically proven to be imperfect. I mean a believe system created out of sense organs will more often be negative in nature and manifest negative things in our reality. Thus, spiritual focus is always to control the sense organs and believe in things beyond it. Lord Hanuman is also called *Jitendra (Jit-Endra)*, you might have heard this word so many times but never thought about its meaning. Simply, *Jit* means Win/Victory and *Endra* means *Indriya* or the sense organs. One who has achieved victory over his sense organs is a *Jitendra* and you have already by now understood how flawed sense organs are and how believing in things gets manifested. Thus, the core essence of spirituality, knowing self and knowing the reality is winning over sense organs and when you do so, you will be able to believe and manifest anything supernatural.

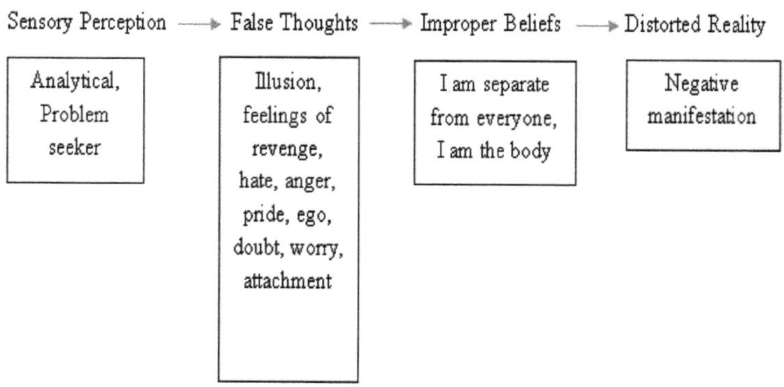

The above diagram helps understand how a flawed sensory perception leads us to create a negative state of reality, a negative state of being. That's why we see people with all sort of luxury and still suffering from depression. Rich crying for peace, poor crying for money, people who have work crying about work pressure, people who don't have work begging for employment opportunity, people who don't get love crying for love, people who get love crying about possessiveness because all these are sensory perceptions and illusion of reality, real joy lies in understanding the real nature of reality and that everything in this world is manifested according to believe.

Reality works hard for laymen

Reality is often considered hard and every aspect of life is considered hard. Pardon my language but fools have ingrained the concept of hard work so much that they equate it to being successful. LMAO. Let's discuss the reality of hard work. What is hard work and how do you measure it? Is there any data and study that shows how many people who have worked really hard have tasted success in life? There are numerous books and scholars who have eulogized hard work simply because it sounds good. Hard work is just a term used as an excuse when someone fails and as a quality when someone succeeds. If one fails, he must not have worked hard, if one succeeds, he might have worked really hard. But there is no one who has actually measured who have worked how much hard. In my personal experience I have seen people struggling and working hard all their lives and achieving nothing while some people have such a calm demeanor and approach to life that they achieve much even without burning themselves out. What role did hard work play then?

In the book 'Don't believe everything you think' the author Joseph Nguyen says that only those desires that are end in themselves bring joy and fulfilment and not those desires which are means to an end desire. Example- If you have a desire to earn a lot of money so that you can lead a luxury life or provide for your family, it will be very hard to earn money because your real desire and joy is something else, money and your job serve as a means to achieving them and thus earning will feel like a lot of hard work being done. As I write this, I am now typing for straight 3 hours and I don't have any other desire at the moment other than to type this book, it is bringing me joy and I am not even feeling a slight drop in energy. I won't call this hard work but to some people typing straight for 3 hours is hard work. Take example of any field, actor, sportsperson, entrepreneurs, all those who followed their passion may work a lot but don't feel a slight drop in energy, they enjoy, they are fulfilled, and they earn a lot, while a corporate layman employee who just works for money always curses his job, because it's not the job or money he loves but what will happen after it. Hard work is only for those suckers. Chairman of Larsen & Toubro says that he loves to work even on weekends, of course that's why he is the chairman for success only comes to those who love what they do not to those who work hard, because working hard by its nature can only be felt by those who don't love their work.

I will discuss another nuance; it's not hard work that brings success but work with believe and passion. I couldn't have typed for so long if I didn't love writing. In commercial education we are taught that there is an external environment which a business organization cannot control at all, now tell me if a layman gives 100s of hours of hard work and some element of external environment always goes against him, how will he be successful? On the other hand, a passionate person who just loves his job, keeps working without thinking much of the result, having a positive believe and faith, will surely achieve success. How? Firstly, Since he loves his work he can keep going on without fatigue and hard work, second, we have learnt in previous chapter about law of attraction and how positive faith and not thinking much about results align our vibration and body language to our external environment, thus external factors will also start working in his favour and thus, since his desire is the job itself and not what he is getting from it, he will experience fulfilment and growth which any hardworking layman wont experience in his lifetime and with this fulfilment and growth abundance and luxury comes naturally. Many might say that if a person works hard, luck will automatically favour him, that is untrue. If you observe carefully, almost every other person works hard so it's not basically that hard work is what creates luck but the positive believe system of a person and a positive believe system related to work can only be found in people who love their work and here is the paradox, the people who love their job will never feel like they are working hard. They might feel tired but never burnt out. Hard work is also a very negative term. If our believe creates our reality and we always believe that work is hard, work will remain hard forever and no success will be achieved. Plot twist, most of the corporate layman or anyone who work for money, will feel work as hard forever because it is not the job they love but what they get from the job and to such people abundance would hardly ever come.

One yet Many

The nature of truth is such that there is nothing true or false. Reality is one yet many, God is one yet many, I am one yet many. Monotheists disagree with Indian and eastern philosophies for being polytheistic. They say God is one and only that God should be worshipped. I will say those people have failed to understand the concept of perception. I have already said that God is one so I am not disagreeing to any religion but people who fight to prove their view of God lack the knowledge of perception. I would illustrate this topic through my own story.

My name is Sa**n**yam, (emphasize on the n). I am a 23-year-old man with finite qualities, attributes and characteristics. I have met thousands of people in my life. Due to the silent n in my name, some have pronounced it as Sannam, some have called me even Samyan, some called me Shyam while some have called me Saiyu out of love while some friends call me Sam. Now out of these people who have called my one name in so many different ways some met me when I was a weak fragile young kid, some met me when I was strong adult working out every day, some met me when I was feeling down and despondent at work, some met me when I was shining at work, some met me as their lover and saw the childish side of me, yet some are reading this book and seeing a mature side of me. If you pick any of these persons and ask them to define me, they will define me very differently and yet all are true. Such is the nature of reality and God. If I as a normal human being with finite qualities can have so many different images in people's mind imagine how many perceptions of God (who has infinite qualities) people can have. That is what monotheists don't understand, no culture says that God is multiple, we say perception of God is infinite and each human being is entitled to have his own perception of God and yet each of them will be completely true because in the cosmic world there is nothing wrong or right. Such is the nature of reality as well. Jainism teaches the same in the concept of *Anekantvada* or no real absolutism. Refer my example again, if each of the person I met starts fighting among themselves that what they know of me is the only truth they will never know the complete me, but if each of the person I met start sharing their experience of me and add each of their experience in a chronological sequence, they will get to know me inside out. Similar is the case with God, my disagreement with monotheists is not when they say that they believe in one God, my disagreement is when they fail to understand the science of human perception and that God with infinite qualities may show different versions of himself to different people and thus form a different image in the mind of each devotee and thus each devotee is entitled to that different image. Similar is the working of reality.

By now you must have understood how nuanced reality is and how much illusion of reality is created by our own logical brain working through the sense organs. This is not the end to the discussion of reality. In the next chapter, I will share the role of Karma in shaping reality, how karma actually works and spares no one and how the understanding that law of karma means you get what you work for is not fully correct. We will learn what the various schools of spirituality talk about methods of getting rid of accumulated karmas, how actually performing various austerities and control of senses negates or nullify the effect of past karmas. All of it in a very scientific approach and not just layman gibberish.

4

"As a reflection clings to a mirror, so karmas cling to the soul through attachment and aversion."

-Acharya Hemachandra

KARMIC REALITY

The word *karma* means deed or action. As I am writing this book my present karma is 'Writing a book'. Anything that is a verb describes *Karma*. The basic principle of karma known to us is that 'as you sow, so shall you reap' meaning we get according to what we give. In our general experience of life, sometimes we observe that reality is really working according to this principle while many a time we feel that it seems we are not being treated by life in the manner we deserve. The concept of karma in philosophy is very intricate and it does work in every moment of our life. This chapter is aimed at giving a clear picture of how theory of karma actually works and how it is that so many people who have been doing good deeds all their lives still suffer. It will, in a very simple manner, help you understand why the concept of karma is generally misunderstood and not believed by masses. But before going into the concept of karma, it is very important to know about soul or the life energy that resides inside us.

Soul and it's properties

There is a life-giving energy inside all the living organisms in the world. This energy is invisible, just like how radio waves are invisible, and it is a part of supreme cosmic energy observing the entire universe which in general words we call God. All the modern invention we see in our day to day lives – buses, cars, airplanes, computers, mobiles, elevator etc., all of these run on an energy called electricity, a car may need petrol or diesel but what does that petrol do? It converts into electricity to help run the car. The base of all the modern technology is electricity. Now I may ask what is an electric current, it is the free flow of electrons from a region of higher potential to a region of low potential. If you have not studied physics, let me explain this again in simpler terms. Take example of water, if you combine two containers with a pipe and fill one container full with water and have the other container empty, the water will flow from the container which is full to the container that is empty through the pipe. In a similar manner, electrons flow from a region of higher potential (more electrons) to a region of lower potential (less electrons). The difference in the number of electrons between higher and lower potential is what we call Voltage. It means that for electrons to flow there must be a voltage (difference in number of electrons between two region). If two water containers have equal quantity of water and they are connected with a pipe, water will not flow from one container to other because there is no difference in quantity of water (no voltage). Now as electron runs from high to low potential, a thing is created which runs is the exact opposite direction, this thing is called an electric current, which is the life line of all modern technology. Thus, electricity is the soul of modern machines. Those machines which don't run on electricity also needs force from some other source to run, that force is their soul. In a similar manner, all of us the living beings are biological machines which runs all soul. People may die due to a brain stroke or heart failure just like a car which won't work even if it has electric supply if its engine fails. But if the car is completely in a working condition, everything is right, still it won't work if it is not supplied with electricity, similar is the case with us, everything in our body maybe fine till the end of our lives but the day we are deprived of our soul, our body will stop working. Now how soul comes into existence, there is simply no clear answer to it in this realm. Can you answer how light energy came into existence, you may say that we get light from the sun but then how sun came into existence, you may refer to the big bang theory, but then how big bang explosion happened? The only answer is that entire Universe is based on energy and that when we refer to our world, we have a law of conservation of energy that states that – Energy can neither be created nor be destroyed but can be transformed from one state to another. We have studied the structure of atom and we know how sub atomic particles like electrons, protons etc. carries a charge. Electrons are negatively charged while protons carry a positive charge. Thus, since soul is an energy, it can neither be created nor be destroyed, it can be channelized, and it carries a charge. The rudimentary thing in understanding the working of the theory of karma is that soul carries a charge.

Now what is the structure of a soul. We have discussed before about properties of an electric current. So, soul must also have some properties. The first property is that it cannot be seen, some form of energy can be seen while some form of energy cannot be seen, we have discussed about what we can see and what we cannot in the previous chapter, we can see electric current while we cannot see radio waves. It all depends on the frequency, for example- when the blades of a table fan are still, we can see them but when the fan is switched on, we cannot see them. Soul is a high frequency energy and thus cannot be seen but only be observed, that's why we feel paranormal and talk about ghosts and all near graveyards. Soul by its very nature will never harm anybody but since it's a life energy it needs a living functioning body to express itself and since it also has certain charge so people often feel paranormal near graveyards because there are energies that want to be expressed through a functioning body and the charge which a soul carries is what lead us to actually sense the presence of a soul near graveyards or haunted places. The second property of soul is that it is ever expressive. The soul always wants to express itself and for that it needs a living functioning body, electricity without any device that can help it flow is useless. The third property of soul is that it creates an attachment with the body it is a part of. A soul which has resided inside the body for so long when it is deprived of that body and the astral cord (which connect soul to the body) stops functioning, it still tries to flow into that body and suffer due to its inability to do that. That's why in our culture we cremate the body after death instead of burying it and that is why graveyards feel more intense and paranormal then crematoriums because since the body is completely destroyed in crematorium the soul has nothing left to hover around while since the body is still there in graveyard and gets destroyed slowly the soul energy remains hovering around it. S*hastras* say that cremating gives the soul *mukti* (freedom) from the body. But in our culture, when an infant or a child dies, we bury their body and not burn it. It is not because it feels very painful to see a child body burn (of course it is painful but the reason is not that), the reason is that since the soul has not lived in that body for a very long time, it has not developed an intense attachment with the body and will get easily detached from the body so there is no urgency to destroy the body immediately.

This understanding of the soul and charge is very important to understand the working of the theory of karma, the understanding of law of attraction given in the previous chapters is also very important. That's why we have discussed these topics in such depth. The understanding of the working of human organs like heart and brain and the layers of our environment is also important and we will go through them layer by layer.

Karma, Mind & Reality

Karma → Memory → Thoughts → Beliefs → Body language & Vibration → Reality

Karma	Memory	Thoughts	Beliefs	Body language & Vibration	Reality
Deeds which can be negative as well as positive	Imprint of those deeds, what we felt, our bodies vibration, heat, etc., when we were doing those things	The resulting thoughts that come to us based on everything we do	What our thoughts make us believe about the reality	Our resulting subconscious behaviors and vibrations based on repeating thought pattern and belief system	Final manifestation

We know by now that it is what our believes that shape our reality, that manifests supernatural things in our reality. But we haven't realized yet what our believes are. Do they align with what we want or are they aligning with what we don't want? And more over how our believes are actually formed. We think we believe what appears to us as truth. No, our believes are formed out of a complex system of thought pattern. The chart above summarizes how the chain of our action forming our reality goes by. It isn't a physical chain but a mental chain. It starts with us engaging in a type of deed and action, then we form a memory of everything related to that deed, action and event. In our thoughts, then, we experience the same deed or events related to that deed again and again. A neural community is formed in our brain and through a complex repetition of the said things, beliefs are formed. Now we have already studied before that how beliefs affect our body language, vibrations and chemical events and ultimately creating a reality for us. Thus, the starting point is always the deed we are engaged in, that is our karma and the working of the karma theory happens through us internally and not outside us.

Like any curious person, you should now ask that if deeds create our reality in such a way, then why there are people who are constantly engaged in doing good things for others but still never get any abundance in return. There are two answers to it. First, it's not the deed but the motive behind the deed that matters, if someone does good things for other with an intention of self-gain, his memory and thoughts will be created like he lacks such a thing. A lacking thought pattern will create a belief in lacking and eventually the lack will be manifested in reality and he will not get anything even after engaging in good deeds. That is why, culturally it is said 'if you are doing good for others to get something in return and not for the joy doing good deeds bring, you are not doing any good', a businessman whose goal is to solve a problem and not just to earn money often establishes a big business empire. You may now say that many people who really do good with no intention of gain also many a time do not receive anything in return. True. This is the second answer, and in this answer the entire properties of soul we read earlier will come into play. I have said earlier that since soul is an energy it carries a charge; the charge may be positive or may be negative based on the deeds done by the soul when it was in its previous body. After death, when the soul energy is released, it carries the charge with itself, and since energy is neither destroyed nor created, that soul finds another suitable body for itself to flow through and carries the same charge to it. Thus, in our present life our body is new but our charge is what is carried by the soul from its previous body and that charge may be negative based on the deeds done by that previous body. So, when people who have such accumulation of negative charge, do good deeds now, the energy effect of those good things first goes towards clearing the negative charge blockage, In the figure above, we understood how deeds create reality through our mind but this negative charge carried by the soul remains present in the subconscious memory and affects the belief system even after doing good deeds with good mind. Thus, many people who do good deeds with good intentions doesn't get anything in return because the effect of those deeds first goes towards absorbing those negative charge (karmic cleansing) and finally after years or lives of good deeds, when the negative charge is cleared, the result of good deeds starts to come. There is a similar vice versa for those who never do good deed but gets so much in return. It is because their soul carried a positive charge from the previous body which forms a subconscious memory in the present body, which derives a better belief system and good results. Ultimately, if they continue to do bad karmas or deeds in present life, a day will come when their positive charge will be fully consumed and they will also get the result of their bad deeds. In Hindi there is a saying '*paap ka ghada bhar jane pr naash hoga*' (when the bucket of sins will be full, self-destruction will happen). Keep referring the chart above. It is just that to a layman who has not thoroughly studied the science of karma and mind and soul, it doesn't strike and he keeps questioning why there are people who do good and get nothing in return and there are people who don't do any good and get everything in return. I have tried to answer this silly misunderstanding above. No one is spared by the law of karma. The law of karma, as described above, operates very scientifically and intricately through the various energy fields around us and within us and without any limitation of time and body. That's why to a layman it appears to be flawed because the cause-and-effect relationship is not observed immediately.

Karmic Cleansing

If our deeds have such profound impact on our mind and reality, is there any way to get rid of the accumulated karmic memory in our subconscious mind and thus changing our thought patterns and behaviors so that a better reality is manifested. Yes, absolutely there are ways to get beyond the impact of negative karma. It is what we call meditation and austerity. We live in a world where people try to relate every spiritual practice to the body and not the mind. People fast to keep body healthy, do yoga and exercise to keep the body fit, but all these practices, done in a sensical way, have been designed to clear the subconscious mind from all the accumulated maladies and not letting further accumulation of maladies in subconscious mind. Again, refer to the chart of Karma, mind and reality.

There are several types of austerities- fasting, vow of silence, celibacy to name a few. Hunger, taste, speaking and sex are natural to human beings so many people criticize these spiritual practices of abstinence as illogical. What they don't understand is, just like when you lift heavy weights in gym without having any real need ever to lift them, your body grows, in a similar manner when you teach your mind, the art of control and go out of mental comfort, it grows. Moreover, the flow of karma which we have studied above in the chart also gets altered. Suppose you have accumulated negativity in subconscious through wrong doings; it will somehow affect your beliefs and get manifested as a negative reality. But what will happen when you are used to austerity, you will have a control over your mind which will not let your memory and thoughts become your beliefs and when this will happen all the negative patterns stored in your subconscious will overtime disappear and new positive patterns will start to develop, provided you don't again start indulging in previous negative deeds. In Jain doctrine, this is called as the process of *Karma kshaya* (destruction of accumulated karmic memory in subconscious mind).

Irrational Literature

I, often, used to ask my elders as to why we have to fast and that fasting won't make God happy. I realized later that my understanding of God was very flawed, God is not an entity that is going to give things to you. He is an entity which will help you think and believe positively, the energy of Universe is God and that everything in this world and universe is designed very scientifically, our action, thoughts and beliefs manifest magical reality for us, and believing in God, fasting and performing austerities help us to control our deeds and subconscious memory patterns. When our entire mind is positive, our reality manifests positively. Explaining this much to general laymen mass was difficult and time consuming so the spiritual gurus just advised them to do religious austerities and make God happy and get the reward. Indeed, austerity will give reward and God does exist but following a scientific way. The fear of God only helps the masses to do good deeds and indeed it is essential because not everyone can have the understanding you now have after reading this much.

People don't understand the science of the universe because they first want to see the result and then study about it. They hear few *pundits* saying fasting will make God happy and believe it to be a religious superstition and completely deny it. I agree, saying that fasting will make God happy is non sensical, illogical and irrational. That's why more and more people are becoming atheist because though the *pundits* are saying truth that fasting will give you reward, they are propagating it in a manner which is completely unscientific and layman. These method of instilling fear or love of God used to work when people were not very educated. The modern mass needs a scientific understanding of spiritual concepts such as karma, reality, perception etc. but unfortunately most of the *pundits* are also trained by their gurus using the same layman understanding of the scriptures using literature and metaphors and not science. It is one of the main reasons that belief, faith and concept of God is declining while religious dogmatism is increasing in the world.

If you have studied science in class 6-7 and done PhD in any scientific field. You can notice how much difference in understanding was, then and now. Yet that class 6-7 kid would argue about things quoting science. In a similar way people have very layman understanding of God and they think that their understanding of God is all what the scriptures say, wrong. At the philosophical level scriptures are very scientific but to impart those scientific knowledge gurus used literature and metaphors. The tragedy is that people started believing in metaphors as the literal meaning rather than the actual science which the metaphor was intended to explain, such is the case which happened with the Law of Karma. No doubt now in this world, in every sphere of life, rich or poor, abundant or lack, people are suffering mentally because they are logical enough to understand that God wont reward them (true) but they don't apply much logic enough to understand that though God wont reward them but the universe is designed in a scientific manner and that faith in God and knowing themselves from the inside, knowing and abiding by the law of karma would definitely reward them. They can reward themselves through practicing spirituality. They are logical enough to call out religious dogmatism but not logical enough to understand that religions were propagated through literature and metaphors. So, though adhering to religious dogmatism is wrong at the same time completely denouncing the scriptures without trying to understand them is also illogical.

Heaven, Hell and Moksha

Since we started this chapter with an understanding of soul. Let's end this with exploring the heaven and the hell. We studied in the previous chapter that reality is an illusion and that it is created in our mind through our sense organs. If we don't know anything about heaven and hell, and if our sense organs are imperfect how can we possibly find a place called heaven and hell. No scientist can ever discover any place called heaven and hell because they are simply a version of reality only experienced by the soul. If no one can discover heaven and hell, then how am I writing about them with so much conviction? Because there existed people who mastered their senses and tapped the infinite intelligence through intuition and observed various facets of reality. They documented all their observations in the scriptures. If this sounds non-sense, let me take you to your dreams.

At night, you are asleep, your conscious mind is asleep and your subconscious mind is active. You are having a very weird, horrific dream, a nightmare, you are seeing creature which possibly doesn't even exist. You suddenly gasped and woke up in horror. Now think three things, how can you possibly see a thing that doesn't exist in the world and a thing which you have never even imagined. Second, how horrific it would have been if you were not able to wake up from that dream. Third, can anyone else enter your dream voluntarily? 'No' right, this is what happens in after life, your soul carries a positive or negative charge based on the deeds done by it during various life times, these charge and your soul both are subconscious elements, your soul experiences and feel things after life according to its charge. A negatively charged soul will be caught up in a nightmare like experience and like you can wake up amidst a nightmare, the soul, in afterlife, stuck in a nightmare has no body through which it can wake up and get out of the nightmare. This is what hell is. Heaven exists in the same way for a soul. A positively charged soul, in its afterlife will experience its own charge, a beautiful dream you can call and since soul cannot wake up from a dream without a body, that beautiful experience becomes a place called heaven. In scriptures, both heaven and hell have been vividly described and various types of heaven and hell have been described which a soul experience based on the type of karma and charge. Elucidating each type is not my goal here. I just wanted to give a brief understanding of the concept of hell and heaven and how they exist yet won't ever be found by a living human (except enlightened ones).

In Indian philosophies, God doesn't exist in heaven, the existence of God is in *Baikuntha* as per Hinduism, *MahaVideha* as per Jainism. All these places are not heaven but supreme state of being. In very general language, you read above that a positively charged soul experience heaven through its own charge and a negatively charged soul experience hell through its own charge. Similarly, a liberated soul is one which doesn't have any charge they don't experience any hell or heaven because their mind is free from the accumulation of good or bad deeds. These soul leaves the planet and aligns with the energy of the universe, that is what we call *moksha*. That's why *sannyasis* renounce material world and attachment. Many people argue that instead of renouncing the world *sannyasis* should work for the good of other people. Here comes the contradiction, if they start involving themselves in good or bad karma, they may carry a negative or positive charge after death. But if they clear themselves of all attachment, erase their accumulated negative karma and carry no charge after death, it is only then when they can be free from the cycle of birth and death and attain *moksha*. If this sounds weird, remember, an iron rod which is positively or negatively charged becomes a magnet and keeps attracting or gets attracted while an iron rod that has no charge neither attracts nor is attracted and is in complete liberation. Thus, the *sannyasis* strive to attain the state of moksha after death and so they don't get themselves involved in any welfare activity or any demonic activity.

Guaranteed Happiness

I was fasting for a day and had a wonderful realization. Being a Jain, we don't have anything during a fast and I suddenly had a very intense craving for lemonade. I felt like when I will have lemonade the next day, I will feel immensely happy. The next day after having lemonade, it appeared to me that if I had not observed a fast the previous day, I would never have felt such happiness from just having lemonade because normally I thought that I have very high goals and ambitions, the fulfilment of which could only make me happy.

We plan to buy an apartment or a luxury car or something very high-end and attach our happiness to the fulfilment of those desires. Nothing wrong in that but what I realized is human can feel happy through achieving anything that is unavailable to them. To us a luxury car may appear a very big thing compared to a lemonade but to the subconscious nothing is big, small, good or bad. Human desires work on demand and supply and that is why spiritual masters teach us to restrain from things, we love and which are available to us, for sometime. When I fasted, I voluntarily stopped eating for a day while food was available to me. It created a fake scarcity in my mind and now my mind started desiring food (lemonade in my case) and attached its sense of happiness to the event of having lemonade. When I opened my fast the other day and had lemonade, it felt so good because I had already created a sense of extreme desire for such a basic thing. This is how we all can create happiness. Instead of desiring very high-end things, if we create a fake scarcity of things which are already available to us, creating a craving and desire in our mind, we can immediately feel happiness once we have those things again. I call it as playing with demand and supply of things to alter the desires of the mind so that mind only desires those things which are available easily and thus always attain happiness.

You may say that if we all rely on this method, there will be no development and economy will hamper. My question is that- what will you do of a development and high standards of living when you never get to feel immensely happy? And in fact, if you train your mind to live happy through the fulfilment of these self generated petty desires, with time, your beliefs will start to align with that of a happy and fulfilled person and eventually your vibrations and body language will manifest all the high-end luxury in your life, through the operation of the law of attraction in a way we discussed in the previous chapters. Thus, happiness is guaranteed through this method of abstinence.

5

"Love is the bridge between you and everything."

-Rumi

MIRACLE OF LOVE

We are only ever one thought away from a miracle but out of the infinite possibilities of thoughts, how can we possibly arrive at that thought which aligns with our purpose and which would bring us joy and fulfilment. It is usually not us who arrive at thoughts but thoughts come to us. There is a subtle difference between thoughts and thinking. Thoughts are what come to us subconsciously whereas thinking is what we do through our conscious mind. Thoughts are always intuitive whereas thinking is always analytical. As we already know, we can only analyze things we know thus we cannot imagine new things through our thinking. It is the thoughts which are a product of subconscious build up which provides us a whole new vision of life. Thoughts are what that is sent by God (the vibrational energy of Universe) while thinking is what we do based on our sense organs. I fell for a girl at the very first sight of her, rationally people would say how can you love a person without even knowing them and that it is just an infatuation, an attraction but my point of view here is that I have seen so many attractive people but why I felt this way for that one person only. Loving her is not something that I have to think about but it is something that happens to me naturally. It is like all the sequence unfolded in a serendipitous way to make me meet her. I knew from the very first moment that there is a match, how? Because I didn't have to think anything about her, whether she has values, moral, culture, knowledge and a positive outlook. I knew that she has it all even without talking to her once. I knew all the qualities that I am developing in myself is present in her. Happened what, when I got to know her, everything of mine matched with her- her paternal native, her maternal native, our education level, our spiritual interest, our general outlook-all these may be a co-incidence but then the entire astrology birth chart matchmaking matched, I mean in astrology matchmaking is based on calculations and not subjective assessments and obviously none of us had control over the date we were born. LOL. Stunning thing is that my mother told me a few days back that I was born a month earlier than the scheduled date given by the doctor. It felt as if I was made to appear on the earth at the exact moment when everything of mine matches with her and as I said earlier, I knew that everything matches from the moment I saw her and before even knowing the slightest details about her. Miracle isn't it. This is a very personal and close to heart topic for me and I will not disclose her name here because privacy is what keeps the miracle alive and for me indeed, she is a miracle. I narrated the life event which is closest to my heart just to show how intuition (thoughts without thinking) always shows you what is true and real while thinking will always make you question out of a fear of what will happen in future. Thinking always blocks miracles. If my story appears like sugar coated version of reality. I would quote what one of the greatest minds of our time had to say about intuition vs rationalism.

"The intuitive mind is a sacred gift, and the rational mind is a faithful servant. We have created a society that honours the servant and has forgotten the gift"

-Albert Einstein

Einstein, who has been one of the greatest minds in the field of science, advocates that intuition is always above rationalism. In the context of our life, think yourself how many times while making a decision, you listen to your intuition. Most of our decisions are taken based on the fear of future, or what feels safe, analyzing and consulting thousand times before arriving at it, while the correct decision is already known to our subconscious. Our logical mind seeks comfort and it thinks only what it can predict of the future can help in achieving comfort, but this is completely incorrect because the logical mind has very little knowledge while subconscious is a store of infinite intelligence.

Love and Relationship

Some positive minded people always say that good things for them has already been decided by God and will be sent by Him when the time is correct. I completely agree with this theory but how will you know that the thing that has come to you has been sent to you by God and not by your flawed decision, which may prove to be disastrous. Every year so many people get married- some through an arranged setup while some through love. Some arrange marriages fail while some goes smooth, some love marriages fail while some goes smooth. If everything that had come to you or every relation that you have established has been sent by God then why do so many marriages fail. There shouldn't be any failed marriage, right? The thing is God does decide our fate and does send right things in our way and to find those things, we don't have to put in any effort, they will naturally stay with us but at the same time God has given us all an option whether to accept his gift or trust our logical mind out of fear and choose a flawed person or reality. In an arranged setup, most people go in search of looking for the right person, analyze thousands of things, discuss a lot with relatives, plan every aspect of future and still so many marriages are failing these days, why? Because human choices are being guided by logic and fear rather than intuition and trust. I will not spare love marriages too, many people who have actually fallen for each other based on physical attraction and had never experienced that intuitive hunch may end up marrying but often their marriage fails. There are brighter side to the things as well, many arranged marriages and love marriages end up wonderfully. What I am talking about is the key determinant- if in arranged setup, everything feels effortless, there is no fear, and there is a mutual understanding that the other person will support unconditionally when one of them will suffer in life, that is when you know that the marriage will be successful. Similar is the case with love marriage.

Some might say that divorces in the case of love marriages are way more than divorces in the case of arranged marriages. That may be true. But tell me where is the data that all the marriages that have never ended in divorces are happy relationships in the present. There are so many cases of marital rape, domestic abuse, dowry related abuse, but still, many of those women have to forcefully stay in the marriage because of the fear of the society and their own traditional background. Look at the dynamics of the institution of marriage. Women suffer more than men in any marriage, maybe men have to take up the responsibility of the family and provide for the family but for a woman her entire world changes mentally, emotionally and physically. In our society, women are often questioned about her modesty and purity and that's why most women fear marriage more than any men and that's why in most cases of arranged marriage women have to stay in the relationships even when it is not happy and fulfilling. Love based marriage also have such cases. The only conclusion is that the rate of divorces doesn't give any idea about which stream of marriage is preferable.

To all the men and women reading this, I will advise that never fear, never ever fear anything, how things would go, always choose the partner who understands you and with whom your everything matches. Never fall for societal pressure because society itself is f*cked up. Being practical is normal, looking for whether your partner will be able to provide for you is normal but don't give it that much importance if there is a hunch in you that says you have met your person because one who is broke today might be well established in future and one who is well established might be a future bankrupt. Money and provision are always subjective. You might end up with a person who becomes financially broke and mentally unavailable in future. If love and hunch and intuition is there just go for it.

In previous chapters, I have explained how our thoughts and believes shape our reality. In a similar manner if you have found a potential relationship and looked about every aspect of your partner without that hunch and love and intuition, and agreed to the relationship, you may end up manifesting a bad reality because the basis of your relationship was fear, fear whether your partner will be able to provide you things, and look after you and this fear will always manifest itself in reality. Maybe everything will seem fine and normal in the starting phase but things will eventually turn. Our parents, wish the best for us because they care about us much more than anyone else, but this unlimited care often builds up fear, that's why most parents don't agree to love marriage. Humans want logic in everything so the parents may find a match for you who can provide you with everything and every comfort of life except love and I must say comfort without love is discomfort. I am not advocating to go against the will of your parent's and hurt them. Never do this. I am just saying that as an adult and a human you have a great system of intuition within you, which is directly operated by God, if you have that intuition for a person it means that the person has been sent to you by God, be an adult take your decision and try to convince your parents because even if that person may not have much material possession now, if God has sent him, it has to be for some good reason which will bring harmony in future.

Love is Unconditional

Love is unconditional, if it's not unconditional it's not strong enough. Love is true, if it's not true it's not strong enough. If you ask people, who do they think love them unconditionally and most in the world, most if not all, will answer that their parents love them unconditionally. It may be true; it may be not. My aim is not to demean parental love but only to showcase how strong is unconditional love and where is it found. It has been fed to us as a part of culture that parent's love is always unconditional. But it is not the case. I am not saying that no parents in the world love their child unconditionally. Parents sacrifice a great deal for us but first and foremost condition in parental love is that we are born out of their body. I am going to be a parent one day and I would still say this. If you are a parent and reading this and you love your child just because the child is born out of you, your love in not unconditional. Tell me will you love a child who is exactly the same in thoughts, behavior and manner but not born out of you, in a same way as your own child? You may say that you have sacrificed a lot for your child or anything but at the very beginning it's you who have decided to conceive a child. Unconditional love is when you love someone for the person they are and not for how they are related to you. Even in scriptures and epics, parental love has been placed below conjugal love because conjugal love always arises without any relation of blood. In temples, Lord Ram is always with Sita, Lord Krishna is always with Radha, Lord Vishnu is always with Lakshmi. They chant Radhe Radhe to call Lord Krishna, not Devki Devki, not Yashoda Yashoda. People name themselves Radhakrishna, Sitaram, not YashodaKrishna or KoushalyaRam. Why? Because even the scriptures know that parental love is not always unconditional while love between those who have met by destiny, intuition, hunch and God is always unconditional to the core. You may say that many conjugal partners get separated. It happens when love was not even there at the first place. There was no element of intuition and hunch and yet a relationship was formed. In the case of parental love, ask if they would love you and sacrifice things for you if you were exactly the same person with the same personality and outlook but not born out of them. Some may do, some might never while in case of conjugal love formed out of real intuition and hunch, people sacrifice everything for a person whom they are not associated by birth and whom they have option to not to give. Remember, when you feel like giving, even after having an option of not giving, and you don't expect anything in return, it is what is unconditional love but when you feel like giving because you are attached to a person by blood and have a duty to give and you expect reciprocation, that is not unconditional love. People who have no perspective in life may bash me for saying that parental love in not always unconditional but it is what it is. Only a parent who love their child for his/her personality, is open to guide and correct them without trying to control them, and not because their child is born out of them, is a parent who offers unconditional love. Last day I was checking news stories and found that a father disowned his daughter for marrying against his will (is it unconditional love?). Lastly. whatever I have said about parental love stands true in the case of a child's love for its parents (child here means son and daughter, not young kid), if a child loves his parents just because he is born out of them, it is a conditional love, if a child loves his parents because they inspire him to be a better person, guide him, he loves to serve them and there is no reciprocation stress in the relationship, it is then when we call it an unconditional love. I had a discussion on this topic with a friend who narrated an event where a mother begged mercy for her son even when her son committed a heinous crime. He said that it was an unconditional love of a mother. I humbly disagreed. If it was unconditional, would she have asked mercy for the same person, for the same crime if that person was not born out of her womb? No, right. Then, how it is unconditional love. It was just an unconditional attachment because she carried him in her womb, fed him her milk and watched him grow over the years.

If what I wrote in this section appears rude or bullshit, I will end this section highlighting *BhaktiVedanta* philosophy, in Bhaktivedanta, five ways of love towards God have been defined, in an order of increasing strength, that is first being a not so intense form while the fifth one being the strongest form of love towards God: -

1. **Shanta Ras** (Peaceful Love)- where a devotee sees Krishna as the source of peace and neutrality.
2. **Dasya Ras** (Servant Love)- where a devotee serves Krishna with a sense of duty and devotion.
3. **Sakhya Ras** (Friendly Love)- where a devotee establishes personal relationship with Krishna and sees him as a friend and companion.

4. **Vatsalya Ras** (Parental Love)- where a devotee relates to Krishna with the affection and care of a parent, they see themselves as Krishna's parents and care for him as a parent.

5. **Madhurya Ras** (Conjugal Love)- where a devotee experiences a passionate, unconditional and intense love for Krishna. They relate to Krishna as their soulmate. Remember Mira bai spent her entire life not marrying anyone because she considered Krishna as her husband and is believed to have eventually attained the love of Krishna. Similarly, Radha had conjugal love for Krishna.

From the above it is clear that even ancient wisdom and scriptures consider conjugal love as perfectly unconditional. A parent will always love its child even if it is not unconditional (because the foremost condition is that the child is born out of them) but conjugal love cannot exist at all without unconditionality. The strongest form of love is parental love while the most unconditional form is the conjugal love. We find it hard to admit it because our upbringing is attached to respecting parents for their sacrifices and indeed, they must be respected and taken care off but epitome of unconditionality is not an appropriate way to refer parental love. Moreover, the above forms of love are not inferior or superior to each other. I am not saying parents are inferior to spouse or vice versa. I am talking about the position, intensity and type of love. In *Ramayana*, Maa Koushalya had *Vatsalya Rasa* (Parental love) for Lord Ram, Maa Sita had *Madhurya Rasa* (Conjugal Love) for Lord Ram, while Lord Hanuman had *Dasya rasa* (Servant Love) for Lord Ram. Hanuman is Lord Ram's greatest devotee but the conjugal love of Ram and Sita and its unconditionality became the central point of Lord Ram's life and eventually led him to fulfil his life's purpose. Obviously, all the other form of his devotees also played a significant role but even when Hanuman tore his chest apart, there was Sita sitting with Ram. Such is a position of conjugal love because of its unconditionality. So, my dear readers, always choose a partner with whom you experience unconditionality because you may experience a stable married life with anyone but one who is sent to you by God, with a touch of unconditionality, will always push you towards your purpose in life and with that fulfilment and abundance will come naturally.

How does unconditional love feel?

Heavenly. It is ineffable, yet I will try my best to describe it. I started this chapter with my own story and how I found the person with whom I am connected to intuitively. Do we meet regularly? No. Do we stay nearby? No. Do we have any plan of meeting anytime soon? No, then how do I know I love her unconditionally? Simply because I have no materialistic reason to love her and yet with a clear mind when my thinking stop and subconscious overtakes I know that I love only her and also since I have no materialistic reason to love her, I can never unlove her because if I love her for her smile, one day if she feels sad I may not love her, if I love her for her appearance, a day may come when she gets old and then I may lose my feelings. I call these types of love as conditional. I was able to recognize that my love is unconditional because no matter what her external physical, mental or emotional situation is, my intuitive hunch is always that I love her and I am made for her. This is not a favour I do on her and this is not I want her to be grateful about. I don't crave for her physical presence as much as I adore her mental presence. My experience of her has been miraculous and I feel grateful that I met her. I felt spiritually connected to the world and the greater universe. Even much of my knowledge, observations and experiences which I have shared in every chapter of this book came into my life after I experienced the unconditional love for her. So, in a way I could have never written this book or never be this connected to the wholeness of the Universe if I had never met her. (Remember in the last section I mentioned how unconditional love pushes us towards our purpose in life)

There will never be an element of ego, pride, revenge, lust in this relationship because unconditionality brings singularity. In meditation, the goal of a meditator is to achieve oneness (singularity) with God or Universe, that can only happen when there is an element of unconditionality. There are people who complain about how God never gives them things they deserve and also there are heartbroken lovers who complain that they never got the love they deserved. All of these are because they have never experienced oneness with God or their love. The only time I felt weak was when I was thinking about how will I endure life if I get disconnected from her due to any reason. It was not a very good feeling but after some self-reflection I realized that my love for her makes me feel singular and one with her, that anyone to whom I feel one with will always be within me mentally. I now feel her in myself and that's what fulfilment feels like. That's what unconditional love feels like. I can go on to write more and more but let's now move on to the next section.

Love and Miracle

Till now I have discussed about love in relation to various relationships. Once you have experienced unconditional love, the power of love grows in you exponentially. You will now feel love towards everything and anything in life. The old negative thought patterns will breakdown, a positive outlook will start guiding you and this is how you will be directed towards the real purpose of your life. By essence, a human soul is meant to love everything and fear nothing, this ability is seen in an infant (a child between 0-2 years of age) and science says that human mind develops the most when a person is in his infancy. Did you see the connection? During infancy when a child doesn't know any logic of this world, stays in the present moment, cries when it gets hurt, smiles when cheered upon, and experience the unconditionality of love, it is during this phase that its mind grows the most. In fact, if you sit down and compare, entire spiritual practices are aimed at going back to the same state of infancy.

Infant	Spiritual Practitioner
Eats less.	Eats less.
Always in present moment because it doesn't know any logic. So cannot fear or think about future or past.	Meditate and tries to control sense organs so that all the logic is forgotten and mind remains in present.
In a state of observation, learns new things every day.	In a state of observation, experiences visions beyond normal humans.
Scientifically, the mind expands the most during this stage.	A stage like infancy is created and mind expands.
Unconditional love and fulfilment are experienced.	Unconditional love and fulfilment are experienced.
Thus, a miraculous stage.	Thus, a miraculous stage.

People who don’t experience love have forgotten love and have become a logical adult. Magic, love, unconditionality and miracles are only observed when logic is renounced. That is why hardly people experience any love in this world these days because as we grow up, we think that logic is of paramount importance. Logic only brings insecurity, trust issues, fear of losing in the case of relationships while fear, anxiety and worry in the case of overall experience of life. I experience joy, fulfilment, love, growth and harmony because I have renounced logic in life and no matter how mature my outlook and knowledge is of the world. I choose to appear childish in front of my love and be playful and unconditional with her. I enjoy talking to her and engaging with every experience life brings to me. All I would say is ‘my love - you are a miracle’, ‘my life-you have been a miracle’

6

"The most important principle of environment is that you are not the only element."

-Tirthankar Mahavir Swami

MAIN CHARACTER ENERGY

There is a joy in being yourself but this joy is hindered by the non-recognition of yourself as the main character of your life. The protagonist of the story drives the plot forward through his actions but he himself is unaware of the plot. On the other hand, the audience always knows that the story is revolving around the protagonist and will most probably end on a happy note. This fact is also unknown to the protagonist. In a story, the protagonist has to face so many adverse situations, not contemplated before, and all these delights the audience because the audience knows that the entire script has been written to synchronize events and results in favour of the protagonist, the main character of the story. It is always delightful to watch how the various events synchronize in a miraculous way to favour the main character. We are living the story of our lives in first person perspective and we are also unknown to what may happen in the future. We are driving our own plot but often due to the adversities life put on us and the logic we apply to it that we start fearing about what may happen and forget that we are the main character of our lives and just like in every story, we have a purpose to fulfil in this life and maybe this purpose is yet unknown to us but it will be revealed to us in a serendipitous way. The purpose can never be to earn a lot of money, make a fortune because money is a very subjective thing and the value of money is always dependent on human demand. In fact, the fulfilment of our life purpose often brings us money, fortune and abundance effortlessly. The first and foremost thing for us to recognize is that we are here to live a life of purpose and believe that through all the adversities, we the main character of our lives are being guided divinely for the accomplishment of our life's purpose. Often, during these adversities is that most people forget that they are the main character of their life and instead employ their rational and go against the normal flow and script of life. They spend their entire life without fulfilment of their divine purpose and then vouch about the hardships of the life on earth. At last, they are eliminated from their own life itself without any material achievement just like if during the shoot of a movie, the lead actor continuously disregards the script or improvise to the extent that the very purpose or aim of the movie is altered, he might be removed from the project altogether. This chapter aims to bring back the main character energy in you and will discuss how can we go through life without disregarding the divine script written and directed by God or the Universal energy, how can we understand the divine direction of God and also, when we feel like improvising the script, how can we do that without altering the very purpose of our life script. It will help us in understanding how can we complete the movie of our life without being eliminated from the project and enjoy the success, recognition and abundance it brings when the purpose of the movie is recognised by the wide audience, in our case, when the world around us is finally benefitted from the fulfilment of our life's purpose.

Recognition of self

In a general sense, the word ego carries a negative connotation, suggesting a self-centered, arrogant and apathetic personality. The word ego in its literal meaning means a person's sense of self-esteem or self-importance. Not only does a person with a superiority complex has ego but also a person with an inferiority complex possesses extreme ego. A person can only suffer from inferiority complex or have a superiority complex if he has a sense of self-esteem and self-importance. It is where the sense of self is leading a person is what decides his complex. A person can only feel inferior if he attaches extreme importance to himself and is unable to meet his own expectation of importance. The word 'ego' is a very neutral word. In Sanskrit, ego is translated as ***'ahankara'*** which is formed out of two words 'aham' and 'kara'. Aham means 'me' while kara means 'action or doing'. So, anything that recognizes and limits you to your body and not to the soul and inherent energy is ego. A person, who may not gloat about his achievements or have no achievement at all, be in a miserable state and always consider everyone to be superior than him is still a person possessing ego because to 'me the body' is the foundation of ego, inferior or superior is the result of ego. In spiritual realm, it is advised to do away with ego and most people interpret it as just to not consider themselves superior. It is where they go wrong, to do away with ego means to not to put themselves into the scale of judgement, to not recognize themselves as either inferior or superior and it can only happen if you stop recognizing yourself as a physical body and introspect within to tap the energy of your soul. Superiority complex is found in very few people while most people consider themselves inferior in some aspect or other. When it is advised to let go of ego, these people with inferiority complex think that they have no ego and thus, this advice is not for them but if they actually realize the meaning and working of the word ego, they will realize that all their inferiority complex was born out of their own ego and that if they let go of their ego, they can actually feel more whole and equal to others.

Some may ask- How can a person live without any self-esteem or self-importance? – My response is- Why not? What made you think that a person cannot live without self-esteem or self-importance? Self-esteem and self-importance are always dependent on external validation and anyone who thinks that they can't live without it have actually never really lived. Imagine what life would feel if you have nothing to prove to others, nothing to chase but you already have everything proven to yourself. It will not be boring because when you have nothing to prove to others, you will have all the time for yourself, to do work that makes you feel whole and engaged, and ultimately this very thing will lead you to find the true purpose of your life. For example- If you are attaching self-worth to display of richness or money, you may never get that money or even if you get and you flaunt wealth, people may not give you that much attention as you were craving. Your whole life will pass away in this and you will never feel whole. Ironically, people call this life exciting while the one without this as boring. I am writing this book and I feel whole and fulfilled, there are people who are doing

9-5 jobs and they may also be feeling whole and fulfilled. I am not saying that people should leave their job and roam around finding their purpose. All I am saying is recognize yourself apart from the ego, do the job in which you feel whole and not in which you don't feel whole but which feels necessary for you to prove things to other or chase self-worth. Never do that thing.

Source of energy

When the veil of ego has been uplifted and real purpose has been identified, energy will come to you inherently. This energy is what which will make you feel like a main character. Thus, the name of the chapter is- 'Main character energy'. Not only will this energy make you feel empowered, whole, fulfilled and exuberant but it will also radiate out of you and will be felt by people around you (aura as it is said). The questions that arise here are- how? And what is the source of this energy? It is simply the mental energy which you have saved by not engaging much in the activities which were making you feel unwhole and unfulfilled. You have saved mental energy by not engaging your mind much in the effort of proving things to others or proving things to yourself, or chasing things. Try for yourself. Let go of your ego, redefine your sense of self and do activities that makes you feel fulfilled. You will find yourself full of energy which is nothing but the mental energy conserved. It is not that how mentally or physically laborious the work is which makes us feel tired but it is actually how much our interest and inner calling for that work which decides whether we will feel tired after a day full of work. A person who loves, suppose, a finance job may not feel tired or stressed or anxious even after working for 15 hours a day and I have personally met such a person while I have also seen people complaining about their job even after getting all the benefits associated with it and working for a normal 8-10 hours a day. Such people criticize everything about their job, even after getting a good salary, they remain ungrateful about the opportunity they have got while so many others sit unemployed and desperate for a job. All these are because the only thing they want from their job is money. I am not saying that no one should speak against the management in case of discriminatory and unfair treatment but stop cursing your workplace for work if it's you who don't like the work and have still chosen the job. Either leave it or if you are in dire need of money, be grateful that you have that job.

The source of all energy is God and what is God but the energy that observes the universe and the energy that is inside you and me. Finding God is about finding yourself, when you have really understood that it is ego (sense of self) which makes you feel either superior or inferior, and that these feelings make you feel separate from others and incomplete, if you let go of the ego, you will easily connect to the energy inside you and feel that nothing inside and around you are flawed. When you have felt such an energy, who can possibly make you upset? No one. This is how God is the source of all energy.

Driving the plot

When you start feeling fulfilled and exuberant about your job and things you are engaged in your daily life, you are already now aligned with the divine script of your life. Everything that is happening in present will drive you towards the various plotlines of your life. You will never know when and what and how things are getting synchronized but your job is only to stay aligned with the main character energy which we have discussed in the previous paragraphs. Since, events are always synchronized and a stagnant stage may be a part of preparation for a bigger event, there may come a time when things become stagnant and you start to doubt whether whatever you are doing is right or wrong. Do not deviate from your path during this period of stagnancy. It is during this period that you should talk to yourself as the main character and realize that the hero or the heroine never know how things are synchronizing but eventually continuing to follow the script that had started with making them feel whole will always lead to a perfect ending. Calm logic and embrace the magic. The plot will pass, the climax will flow and a perfect result will appear. The timing would be unknown but that is what the magic is. I can say this with full conviction because I have experienced the working of it in my life. If you too sit and retrospect your life, you can relate so many events which you desired and felt whole about and they happened magically and you felt more aligned and fulfilled. The main character will always win but it is on you to embrace the energy of the main character and tell to the universe that you are ready for its plans.

Improvising the Script

During the shoot of a scene or a theatre play, actors sometimes deliver dialogues which weren't originally the part of the script. If such improvisation serves well for the situation, theme, the character and the overall scene, it is accepted and the story goes ahead otherwise the scene is shot again. In life also we can improvise certain things according to our situation provided that our improvisation doesn't go against the synchronization that the divine script was trying to execute. We can obviously do anything in life even if they go against the divine script but in life, there are no retakes. Once we deviate from the script and fail to recognize the deviation, we might end up with an unfulfilled life and ultimately be removed from this life. In previous paragraphs, we have learnt how to recognize and be aligned with the script and flow with it. Improvising a script without altering the basic nature of it encompasses taking decisions of life that aligns with the objective of making you feel more whole, purposeful and exuberant. It will not make you feel unaligned and won't consume your energy or lead you to some materialistic pursuit. For example- a decision based out of greed will definitely make you feel unaligned because hundreds of future scenarios will be played in your mind which will consume a lot of mental energy and even if the greed is satisfied it will feel pyrrhic and won't let your mind settle and enjoy wholeness. It is at this moment you should realize that your earlier decision was not an improvisation of divine script but alteration of it. This is the case with so many people who even after building a fortune end up in a very miserable mental state because what is money but an object of external validation. When you have built a fortune and have tasted all the external validation, felt secure regarding the materialistic side of the life, what is that which makes you feel restless? It's the non fulfilment of your actual purpose. That's why many rich people say that money is not important. The poor and middle class, often, disagree to it but they don't realize that even they desire money only to survive and enjoy certain things. After the survival, enjoyment and flaunting part is done, what will be left? A time will come when they will realize that though money is necessary but more necessary thing is what they should have done with the money which would enable them to die with extreme peace (that is the fulfilment of divine script and purpose which can only be felt and experienced by each person).

Affirmations

I would like to end this chapter with some affirmations and examples that all of us can use in our daily lives to always be connected with the learnings of this chapter:

-

- As a soul, I am a part of the Universal energy and thus I am the main character of my life. I don't recognize this body and I am neither superior nor inferior.
- Anything that is bringing me inner joy, peace, calmness and empathy for self and others is aligning me with the flow of my life and directing me towards my purpose.
- I have no revenge to seek, no person to prove, no goals to chase. I am whole and fulfilled in

the process of what I am doing without expecting any result. (many people think that revenge acts as a motivation but after the revenge part is done what will you do of the thing you used to take the revenge, that's why don't pursue a goal just because it will help you prove yourself to others or seek revenge)

- I enjoy life and every aspect of it. If something bad is happening to me, it is forming a part of the sequence of events which will ultimately lead me to real fulfilment.
- Since, I am the energy capable of everything. Nothing is impossible for me. (If I desire to buy an apartment, I already have it in my script. I don't have to be desperate about it. I will just continue to be aligned with my purpose and at an appropriate time I will be introduced with the ability to buy that apartment).

7

"The heart has its reasons which reason does not know."

-Blaise Pascal

ODDS

Everything has a certain odd of happening and my aim while writing this chapter is not to present a scientifically calculated chance of some random events. We have stressed highly upon the power of believing and understood how beliefs manifest reality but even after knowing this, it is very hard to believe in something positive when we are going through a turbulent emotional environment at present. Basically, it is because we are trained to be analytical and logical since childhood and even when we now know that we can manifest what we choose to believe without a pinch of doubt, we have a hard time believing as the mind always questions 'how?' It is during these stressed situations that, at times, even after knowing the science of the universe we choose not to rely on this acquired knowledge and try to control things based on what is visible to us. The urge to control everything and rely on logic is so ingrained in us that it takes over us and get us stuck in the quagmire of manifesting negative version of reality. This chapter won't talk about any science or method but specific viewpoints that enable us to shred the burden of stress and future and completely focus on present because these very things are pre-requisites for inculcating positive belief system. Knowing and practicing are whole different paradigms and thus the aim of the chapter is to provide direction to those who are ready to practice the methods and learnings given in this book.

Things happen

For me, what is the odd of you picking up this book to read? What is the odd that any person who has started to read this book will reach till here? For you, what are the odds that you succeed in whatever goals you have set for yourself? If you strive to calculate the odds, you may find some astonishingly low figures but yet good things happen to so many people effortlessly. In the realm of sports, you might have observed that a player who is going through a lean patch and who is trying very hard to regain his form, often gets to see even the basic things going against him. In cricket, the opponent fielder takes a surprisingly magnificent catch of a batsman who is going through a rough phase while the best fielder drops a silly catch of an in-form batsman. As the saying goes- luck favours the brave, but how and why? All the odds are related to the mutual manifestation of people working through their own mind, belief and behaviour and then an external reality is created, synonymous to the mutual belief. A player going through a rough patch, must be thinking a lot, thinking encompasses analysis and use of extreme logic. As understood in previous chapters, that higher the use of logic, higher mental energy is consumed and no space is left for the divine flow. It affects the body language and movement of the player and finally external things synchronize to manifest reality according to his doubts which were the basis of his analytical thoughts. That's why even after playing some good shots, it happens that the opponent fielder takes some extra ordinary catch. The exactly opposite phenomenon happens when an in-form player plays some silly shot but which even the best opponent fielder drops by chance. People, often, enquire that if beliefs can so easily control external reality than can you see a rock and turn it into foam using your belief and visualization. The answer is no. Why? Because things in our external environment which are not at all related to us have been manifested by the collective beliefs of all the people on earth. A rock will always be a rock and will always hurt you if you get hit by it, because the properties of the rock are based on the collective observations and beliefs of all the humans on earth. What you can control through your belief is never to have anyone to throw that rock upon you or never to get stumbled by a piece of stone while walking. I have been often asked that if believes can shape reality, can you make the sun disappear. The answer is no; the Sun is an infinitely large mass of energy than an average human. When we say that our believes shape our reality, we are not talking about some magic but a science of quantum and energy. It runs on principles which are not physically visible but are observed. Sun can be made to disappear if all the possible living substances in our solar system stays at present moment and accumulate and direct all their energy into believing that the sun is non existent. This sounds irrational but no this is not irrational. Only thing irrational is that, we can never make all the living organisms in the solar system to believe something at the same moment and in the same way. Thus, sun can never be manifested to disappear. Remember, to transform an energy or a mass of energy, we need an even greater channelization of energy. Thus, universal things can never be altered. People generally consider the law of attraction and manifestation as something magical while these laws operate through energy and works on principles. People who refer them as absurd and want some experiment to prove them are ignorant. I mean, how can you make 100 people sit in an experiment and document their believes and their reality after some time. It can never be done because you can never know who believed in a thing how much and how much was the quantum of doubt in their mind. If to you too, this sounds absurd, you can well experiment with yourself. Believe in a thing without any doubt, don't attach a time period and don't attach importance to your belief, don't be excited about the result and don't spend your days thinking about what may happen. Just believe with pure belief without analysis and excitement and importance and I assure with 100% conviction that your beliefs will manifest. After reading this, if you retrospectively view your life, you will observe this phenomenon in so many things or events that have happened in your life. Thus, things happen and odds turn in your favour.

People who experiment with law of attraction try to take control of the law and thus fail. They think that thinking about something all day would manifest their desires. If it was so simple everyone could have done that but it's belief without thinking, attaching importance and without a pinch of doubt that manifests your dominant desire. That's why many people who try to manifest a specific person, a job, wealth, a car or apartment or anything fail because they attach importance to their desires. This is a paradox since you have started to practice and apply law of attraction, you get excited about the possible miracles that may happen, you consume all your energy in thinking and visualizing and with this energy drain happens and mind starts to feel tired. After sometimes, the mind gets frustrated and starts doubting if at all these things works. With an element of doubt, believe loses its potential and instead of your desires getting manifested, sometimes, a completely opposite scenario gets manifested in reality. Thus, things happen and odds go against you.

Neither question nor attach importance

Once you have set out to practice this art and you are experimenting with any of your desire. Don't do the basic mistake of attaching importance to the thing you desire neither doubt about its fulfilment. In short, you have to stop thinking. Start with visualizing what you want, completely being in the present and feeling the energy of what you want and then completely stop thinking about it, attaching importance to it or trying to interpret the synchronicity of events that might lead to the fulfilment of the desire. It relates to two fundamental principles. First, when you attach too much importance to an event, you can never stop thinking about it and we have already discussed in previous chapters that thinking by its nature is deliberate and negative. It also starts occupying a large space of your mind and consumes a lot of mental energy. Thus, no space or energy is left for manifesting your desired reality. Secondly, when you question too much regarding the synchronicities of the event, you again end up with your logical mind forming multiple scenarios and predicting 'what can go wrong'. This leads to frustration, impatience and consumes a lot of mental space and energy. Again, no space and energy remain for your desires to get manifested. Most people who have learned basic law of attraction or energy don't understand these rudimentary principles and end up unfulfilled. They, then, vouch against the working of the law.

How are prayers heard?

If you study any religion or get in touch with its practitioners or proponents regarding your problems. You will find that each of the religion will have certain rituals or pilgrimages or amulets which are believed to work miraculously in solving various problems of devotee related to any aspect of life, be it health or financial or relationship problems. Generally, people call them superstition but yet they have worked out well in several cases. The catch is whenever there has been an attempt to prove their working, it had come out to be false. I can vouch to you that they work. They work for only those who believe without a pinch of doubt. The power is within those believers and not in the rituals or pilgrimages or amulets. Those rituals or pilgrimages or amulets only serves as an external element to create an element of belief in the mind of a person and if that person really believes in their working without attaching much importance or question, their desires are often manifested. This is the prime reason why no scientist or study of science can ever prove the sacredness of any ritual or pilgrimage because they work through belief and through the mind of the person itself who believes. They induce the working of the law of attraction. Even if a person who has been a life long proponent of any religious ideology, has a pinch of doubt in his believes that certain things may not work out, those things will never work out no matter how much he has prayed externally.

Whatever I have said is not based on my own imagination, I will highlight some religious quotes that support what I have said above. Following is the verse from the New Testament – 'Therefore I tell you, whatever you ask for in prayer, believe that you have received it, and it will be yours' (Mark 11:24). This clearly means that it's not the object you are praying but the believe with which you are praying is what which yield results. I respect every religion and have found various meaningful and life changing teachings in every religion. Only reason people are going away from religion is that most of the people have forgot the core teaching, working and philosophy of religion while taken their religion and culture to their ego. My God is only true God- this is the most bullshit thing to preach, because God is everyone's and He appears to everyone in different way and image. The above verse from the Bible itself elucidated how belief is important rather than the bare act of praying. We all pray in different languages, do you think God knows human's languages. God is a Universal energy and when we believe in a thing, our entire vibration and body language get attunes to the feelings related to that belief. When this happens the energy around us gets impacted by the vibrations inside us and shape our actions according to the things we are manifesting. That is how the Universal energy or the God hears and fulfil our wishes. If you are a Hindu who doesn't believe in Bible and the verse I quoted above. Let me give you a quote from your own philosophy- 'God is always within the control of his devotee' (*Bhagat ke vash me hai Bhagwaan*), this directly supports the fact that it is the devotee who can control the energy called God through it's believe. People have forgotten all these elements and consider God as a very high energy separate from themselves. They spend their time believing that everything negative is happening to them and when their own negative energy and belief gets channelized by the Universal energy, manifesting harsh reality, they either blame God or completely deny his existence. At first place their own believe system was flawed. It is your belief and resulting vibrations and body language that communicates subconsciously with everything around you and not just words. Thus, belief is the language through which prayers are heard and answered. A person who has been religious and prayed his entire life to God but always believed himself to be unlucky will be blessed with a reality that is unfortunate. That's why pray consciously and believe very judiciously and positively.

The chapter was meant to provide some real perspective into the minds of the readers who are actually trying to practice the working of the law of attraction in their lives to improve their life's situations. Once you have learned and applied the principles highlighted in this chapter, you will stop worrying about the 'Odds' of happening of various desired events, stop being impatient and eventually start to see the odds turning in your favour. My best wishes are always with you. Believe, Become.

8

"Sleep is the best of physicians."

-Thomas Carlyle

ELIXIR OF SLEEP

Our body is an intricate biological machine capable of regulating various internal cycles on its own. The circadian rhythm is the body's internal clock that regulates sleep-wake cycles, body temperature, hormone release and other biological functions but before we go ahead, why are we even discussing something which is inherent in all of us? Sleep is normally viewed as a state of rest which replenishes our energy and heals every aspect of our being. It is our very own healing process known to us from the very first day of our being. It is indeed sad that our generation has forgotten the magical art of sleep that is the most rudimentary and powerful healing process of our body. According to an estimate around 30% of adults have difficulty in falling asleep and around 10% of adults suffer from chronic insomnia. People attribute highly stressful life situations as the reason for problems in falling asleep but isn't sleep the very process designed to calm and heal the body mentally, physically and psychologically. My purpose behind writing this chapter is to develop an understanding of the working of the circadian rhythm and sleep in our body so that people realize how easy it is to sleep and heal. It is mostly our own resistance that hinders our sleep and we will discuss how to overcome those resistances.

Mechanism of Sleep

The circadian rhythm is nothing but the internal routine of our body working through various organs, glands and hormones. Sleep is induced by the secretion of the pineal gland. This is the gland associated with the third eye chakra and is believed to secrete very powerful metabolites which aid in general healing of the body. It is located deep in the center of brain, just above the thalamus. When we sense darkness and a calm quiet environment, this gland is triggered and secretes a hormone called melatonin in response. This melatonin induces the body to sleep. The sleep occurs in various cycles of two main phases- Non-rapid eye movement phase (N1, N2, N3) and Rapid eye movement phase. N1 is the stage where transition from wakefulness to sleep happens. It is a light sleep stage. N2 is a deeper sleep than N1, here, the heart rate and breath starts to slow down. N3 is the deepest stage of sleep also known as slow wave sleep. In this stage, repair, regeneration and healing of the body happens. Next, the rapid eye movement (REM) phase, which is characterized by increased brain activity and eye movements. Most vivid dreaming takes place in this phase of the sleep. A complete sleep cycle last about 90-120 minutes and a person cycles through this phases 4-5 times each night. When the environment becomes bright and a little noisy, the pineal gland is triggered again and a hormone called serotonin is released which brings the body out of the sleep.

Why people are losing sleep?

You have now got a little bit understanding of the mechanism of sleep. If darkness and quietness is that induces the pineal gland to release melatonin and eventually induce sleep, you can relate yourself that why so many people of our times are finding it difficult to sleep. The mobile phone addiction and advent of very short video content in social media networks which resist the triggering of pineal gland to secrete melatonin. It is not that if you use mobile phones during night, you will lose all your sleep but it will delay the occurrence of sleep and since the body regulates itself through a routine, with time and habit, the body accustoms itself into sleeping late. Thus, we are seeing so many people falling asleep at early morning hours while staying awake at the deepest periods of night. This is a very destructive routine because the environmental vibrations of the early morning hours are similar to the theta-alpha vibrations of the human brain and waking up at that time can actually help in syncing the brain with the environmental frequency. Meanwhile, more and more people are creating a destructive self routine of actually falling asleep at the time when they should wake up from sleep. Thus, we are seeing increase in mental health problems which on diagnosis, are indicating towards no particular disease but still the patient complaints about being frustrated or irritated all the time. We cannot blame a single person as well because the entire system of modern society has been developed as such, especially in highly populated, fast developing country like India. People talk about night life and parties and associate them with the release of stress. Yet countless studies have proven that alcohol is destructive for the human body, that lack of sleep is destructive for the human body, that energy drain is destructive for the human body.

Alcohol And Meditation

By the way, alcohol/drugs (in a general sense) and meditation does the same thing to the mind. Then, why they are bad is because they are external substance whose potency is not in out control. Both alcohol and meditation calm down our conscious mind and thoughts and open the door to our subconscious mind, that's why people feel so good after getting high and that's why they forget everything the next day but alcohol doesn't bring self realization and knowledge because the person doesn't understand what had happen to him. He just goes into a state of non-control and feels extremely good. Eventually, an addiction is created and when the person is deprived of alcohol, he becomes mad and frustrated because even though he had experienced his subconscious but he has not reached there through his own control. Meditation works in a like manner, only difference is that you reach to your subconscious in a very slow and controlled manner and you are open to observation. If you are an alcoholic reading this, just imagine how it would feel like getting high everyday, closing your conscious over thinking mind and just flowing through life without any external substance like alcohol or drugs and all of these in a fully controlled way. This is what meditation brings you about but just like every good thing, it requires practice. Many people who don't know the nuances of mind and meditation, consider meditation as boring but just like exercising is painful but they lead to muscle growth, meditation is boring but cleans and builds your subconscious and heals the body mentally and physically. Once you have tasted the effects of meditation, there is no coming back. All this being said, what is the best time to meditate. Early Morning, the reason being the vibration of the environment being in sync with alpha-theta brain vibration and for this we need to have a natural sleep routine. Now, link everything and you will find why even after the high materialistic standards of living of today's society, there is such a significant increase in the number of mental health related issues. Simply because we as a society have developed so many things for our comfort but we have forgotten that human body is a biological machine that needs to be in sync with its source, that is the nature.

Stress and overthinking

People associate their incapability to sleep with the problem of overthinking and stress. That as soon as they try to sleep, they get caught in the web of overthinking which doesn't let their conscious mind calm and subconscious to overtake into sleep.There are two approaches that helps in solving the issue of overthinking. First, spiritual schools have always advised to pray before sleep. Obviously, the word prayer doesn't appeal to the modern mass. It is that people don't know what is prayer. Praying before sleep encompasses complete surrender of self and ego. When you realize that you are not you, and have surrendered yourself to the Universal energy then naturally you cannot worry about anything. You may be overthinking about what may happen at work the next day or results or contemplating a revenge or some strenuous relationship issues but as soon as you realize that the body is temporary and that you are not the you, you think, all the issues and problems will lose their grip on your mind. This is the best practice to do before trying to sleep. If you think what I have said is absurd tell me what will you achieve overthinking the entire night? First, you will drain all your mental energy, second, since thoughts shape believes and ultimately the reality and logical mind often thinks in negative, a night spent in overthinking would manifest dreadful reality the other day and third, you will develop a habit of living in this miserable way. The easiest way to live whole is to let go of the self, maybe tomorrow, you will have to face some problems but overthinking at night won't solve that instead make them worse, so just for the night, completely dissociate yourself from your body. Believe me, once you develop this as a habit, wonders will happen and you will be able to sleep whenever you want. Healing will flow through you and you won't find yourself separate from any person in your life. This is what we call spiritual awakening.

Sleep Heals

We all are connected to the infinite intelligence through our subconscious mind. This infinite intelligence or field of unlimited possibilities has answers and healings to all our problems. Spiritual masters have achieved command over the subconscious in a voluntary meditative state. A general person's only access to subconscious in involuntary during the deep sleep phase when the brain is in delta vibration state. Thus, sleep is of utmost necessity. It is during this phase of sleep is that answer to every problem is given to us subconsciously and magic happens whether we understand it or not. If you don't believe in the field of infinite intelligence, let me give some examples. Srinivasa Ramanujan, was a revolutionary mathematician known for his contribution in developing the theory of partitions, discovering the Ramanujan prime and Ramanujan theta function and formulating powerful infinite series for pi. He claimed that he had vivid mathematical dreams and that a significant part of his mathematical works including complex formulas and theorems were divinely revealed to him in those dreams. To a layman, this might seem absurd but remember Ramanujan was the first Indian to be elected a fellow of the Royal Society in 1918 by the Royal Society of London. Why would a person of this excellence and intelligence attribute his findings to some mystical dreams? Let's take another example, Albert Einstein reportedly slept at least 10 hours daily and often went to sleep early. Additionally, he employed power nap technique during the day to solve complex problems. He would sit in a chair with a spoon or key. As soon as he starts to drift off into deep sleep state, the object in his hand would fall and the resulting sound would wake him up. This way he could easily remember the vivid imagery of his subconscious mind which was happening during transition phase between light to deep sleep and apply those intelligent images in solving problems. If he had entered deep sleep and had slept for a long period, he would not be able to remember those images formed during the early phase of deep sleep, post waking up. Thus, he used to sleep long during night to heal his body while the power nap technique during the day to tap subconscious imageries. Even in cultural context, it is believed that dreams seen during early morning comes true. People consider it as a superstition because they think it as some sort of magical claim. They don't understand that those dreams are just subconscious imagery of the field of infinite possibilities and if they really tap, interpret and apply the, they can really come true in a subtle way. We have already taken example of the greatest minds of our time to validate the power of infinite intelligence and subconscious mind. Thus, sleep is essential for us to receive divine healing because unlike spiritual masters, a general person can only experience and benefit from his subconscious during sleep.

My own healing story

I was recently diagnosed with severe jaundice and typhoid and was rested in a hospital bed for days. Due to jaundice, I was constantly feeling hungry but vomited instantly on eating even a morsel of food. After series of medical tests, the doctor asked me to not to eat anything until he allows and then I remain laid on the hospital bed for the next few days without eating anything except medicines. I felt hungry during the first day but even the feeling of hunger vanished after the second day. I am a type of person who used to get bored easily and here I was lying on the hospital bed, doing nothing, not reading, not using phone, not eating anything except medicines. Some wonderful realization happened during that time as I began to feel a sense of inherent joy, my sleeping time automatically started aligning with the spiritual teachings. I would wake up at 5 am and fall asleep during the early hours of night. Eventually, I healed after staying there for a week. I know that the doctor's medicines and methods have worked and the part of which was abstinence from entire normal life routine and getting aligned with the routine of nature. I sensed that those sleep I had at that bed were so calm and serene that a large part of my healing should be attributed to the time I spent sleeping there. I stopped feeling bored or irritated easily after that stay at the hospital. Something changed inside me for I have sensed how healing takes place. Something which is very hard for me to put in words but it was the genius of the doctor who aligned modern medicine with natural healing capability of the body and directed me towards healing. I realized that spiritual masters also talk about the very same healing process when they advocate abstinence and fasting, meditation and sleep routine, because in a way the doctor led me to do the austerity of fasting and meditating all day in that bed along with the magic of modern medicines. Before my admission into the hospital, my mother tried so many different ways to assist me in eating without vomiting while I was feeling hungry. All went in vain. She even forced me to eat out of a normal motherly instinct of care and was anxious when I was unable to eat. At last, I healed when the doctor forced me to not to eat anything for next few days. Same thing relates when spiritual masters advocate about austerities, people think that they cannot survive without some basic things like food and entertainment but actually body heals when we let go and rest basic life activities, we experience extreme metal clarity as we get to align with the routine of the nature and thus, we heal. A general person gets anxious on hearing about austerity just like my mother was anxious when I was not able to eat anything. She tried hard to make me eat but healing actually happened when I didn't eat. Our body is a biological self-regulating machine and when it is going against its basic instincts it means it knows what it needs to heal. I was feeling hungry because it was in my routine to feel hungry but my body knew that I need to fast for sometime to heal that's why I was instantly vomiting after eating even just a morsel. Body knows through the subconscious that what is right for it and thus it was constantly vomiting. It was my conscious mind which was making me and my parents anxious as to why am I unable to eat. Similar thing happens during common cold and fever. Body's temperature rises out of its normal immune response to the bacteria or virus but we become so anxious regarding the rise of body temperature and pain that we start having medicine immediately to lower the body temperature which was just a sign of body's response to external germs. In a way, we weaken our own natural immunity by getting anxious and not understanding that fever is natural and should happen so that body fights external germs and heals itself. If you habituate yourself to heal from even the basic germ attack only through medicine, your body will adapt and lose its natural immunity but we as humans always place conscious anxiety and fear over subconscious knowledge and understanding leading to our own harm. All the magical properties and mechanism of sleep together with its association with our subconscious mind and field of infinite intelligence. The healing power of sleep and its role in our survival and self realization makes it nothing less than an elixir that replenishes us with life energy and exuberance. I will end this chapter with few great quotes on the power of sleep.

"Sleep is the best meditation."

-Dalai Lama

"Sleep is the golden chain that ties health and our bodies together."

-Thomas Dekker

"It is a common experience that a problem difficult at night is resolved in the morning after the committee of sleep has worked on it."

-John Steinbeck

"There is more refreshment and stimulation in a nap, even of the briefest, than all the alcohol ever distilled."

-Ovid (Roman Poet)

9

"When I let go of what I am, I become what I might be."

-Lao Tzu

I AM LIMITLESS

Limits exist only in the mind and anything that exists in our mind can cease to exist provided we work on our mind and its basic mechanism. We are coming towards the end of this book and if you have read till here, you know that the entire effort of this book has been towards explaining the infinite potential of human mind and how it is designed in parts to make you forget its own potential capabilities. We, often, find ourselves in extreme situations which makes us despondent and doubtful of our own capacity to handle life. Yet many people have existed in this planet who have achieved such extraordinary feats, even after having very less material and physical resources, as would appear to a normal person as absolutely super natural. This chapter is aimed at sharing ten inspiring stories of people who have achieved extraordinary feats in situations where a normal person would have doubted his own abilities and given up or a situation which a normal person would consider to be impossible to manage. This will aid you in developing an utmost belief in the limitlessness of human potential and since each of us are human, if one has shattered the barriers and limits of the mind and became limitless, it implies that we all are inherently limitless.

- Sheetal Devi, born with a condition called Phocomelia in which arms doesn't develop fully, goes on to become world's first armless female archer, shooting with her feet and ultimately winning two gold medals at the 2023 Asian Para games. Just think how many of us who are blessed with both hands can hit the bull's eye at a distance of 50m even after much practice. Indeed, it was the power of her self belief which helped her overcome the limitations of her mind and body and unleash the miracle inherent in her.

- Ludwig Van Beethoven, who is regarded as one of history's greatest composer, created masterpieces that reshaped classical music despite progressive hearing loss. He continued composing music even after becoming completely deaf in his late 20s. Now try to imagine yourself composing musical masterpiece without even hearing anything. Miracle, isn't it? Limitlessness, isn't it?

- Arunima Sinha, a former Indian national volleyball player, lost her left leg in a train accident. A train went over her left leg, a pain, which even on imagining sends chills down our spine. Refusing to be defeated, she became the world's first female amputee to scale Mount Everest in 2013 at the age of just 24. Sheer will power. Sheer self belief.

- Wilma Rudolph, who was born premature and contracted polio as a child, leaving her unable to walk without braces. She overcame her disability through relentless therapy and determination and became the first American to win three Olympics gold medals in track and field events.

- Rishabh Pant, India's star cricketer, who survived a life-threatening car accident in December 2022 and suffered multiple injuries, including torn ligaments and burns, leaving doubt about his cricketing future. He even asked his doctor if he would ever be able to walk again. Coming to today, he is consistently scoring match winning scores for his team and celebrating his centuries with front flips, wearing all the cricketing gears as if signaling that nothing is impossible if your mind has enough self-belief.

- Nick Vujicic was born without arms and legs. He refused to let his body define him and learned to swim, write and live independently. Today, he is a global motivational speaker, inspiring millions world wide. He is a living proof of the power of determination and limitlessness.

- Hellen Keller was deaf and blind from infancy, faced extreme communication barriers yet became the first deaf-blind person to earn a bachelor's degree. She became a renowned author, activist and speaker. Now think that how can someone who has never heard a word or seen a person learn to speak a language. She learned to speak by feeling the vibrations and movements of her teacher's throats, lips and nose through the Tadoma method. If this doesn't prove you how limitless a human can be, what else can?

- Deepa Malik, paralyzed from waist down due to a spinal tumor, not only pursued a sport but competed in multiple events in para-athletics, winning medals in shotput, javelin and swimming. In 2016, she became the first Indian woman to win a Paralympic medal. Paralysis wasn't able to impose a mental limitation in her mind.

- Nelson Mandela spent 27 years of his life in prison for opposing apartheid in South Africa. Despite the harsh conditions, he never gave up on justice and equality and after his release, became the first black President of South Africa in 1994. You can imprison a man, but cannot cage an idea of justice and equality born out of the divine mind which knows no limitations.

- Franklin D. Roosevelt, who was the 32nd President of the United States of America and who lead his nation through the Great Depression and World War II, had contracted polio in 1921 leaving him paralyzed from the waist down, yet, he pursued a career in politics with unwavering determination demonstrating that courage and vision can overcome any physical limitations.

I have placed the inspiring stories of these ten extraordinary personalities to demonstrate to the readers that how the limitations we perceive in our reality is only created in our mind and that the inherent nature of our existence as a living energy is limitless. Our mind's potential is limitless but just like Lord Hanuman could only use his super powers when he was reminded by someone that he has super natural capabilities, we also need someone to remind us of our inherent limitless and infinite capabilities. Thus, I provided the stories of extraordinary human beings who were just an ordinary human being (with less resources than a normal human being) and who went on to do wonders just by acknowledging and using the inherent limitless energy within them and letting go of the mental blockages.

We all are human and we all have the capability to do wonders. Our capability is hindered by the logic or limits created by our very own conscious mind. This logic and limits, with repetition, gets ingrained in our subconscious to such an extent that most of us can't even recognize potential opportunities and choose to live a life of limitations, misery and blame the supreme energy for our misfortunes. Since, you have read this book, think of this book as a sign from the Universe asking you to believe more in yourself and the supreme energy inherent in you and let go all the blockages created by the logical mind. Now repeat after me as I remind you again of your superpowers -, 'I am the soul, I am energy and I am limitless.'

10

"If I can't picture it, I can't understand it."

-Albert Einstein

VISUAL AIDS

Past and future

Present moment

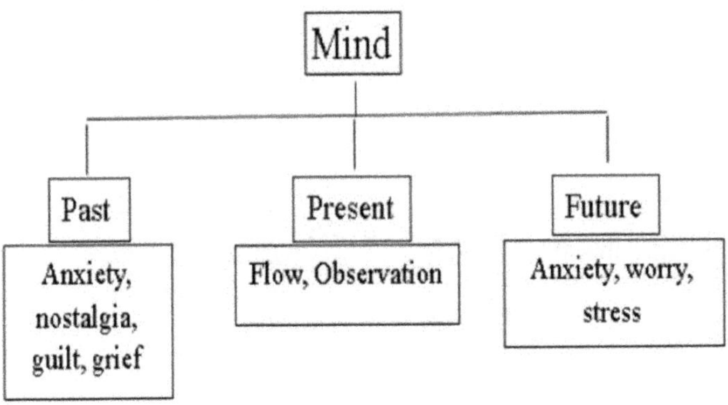

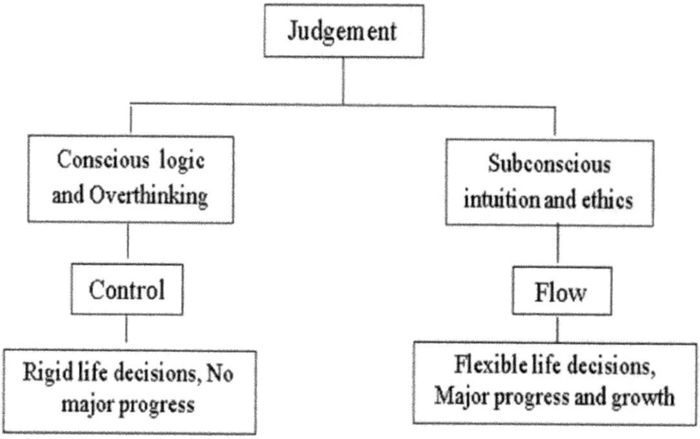
Judgement
Conscious logic and Overthinking
Subconscious intuition and ethics
Control
Flow
Rigid life decisions, No major progress
Flexible life decisions, Major progress and growth

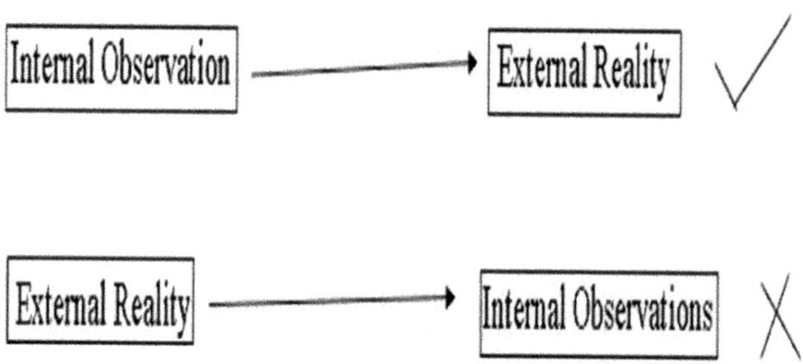
Internal Observation
External Reality
External Reality
Internal Observations

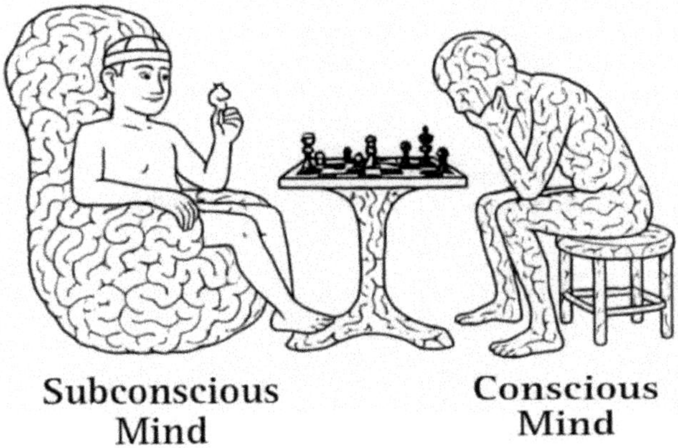
Subconscious
Mind
Conscious
Mind

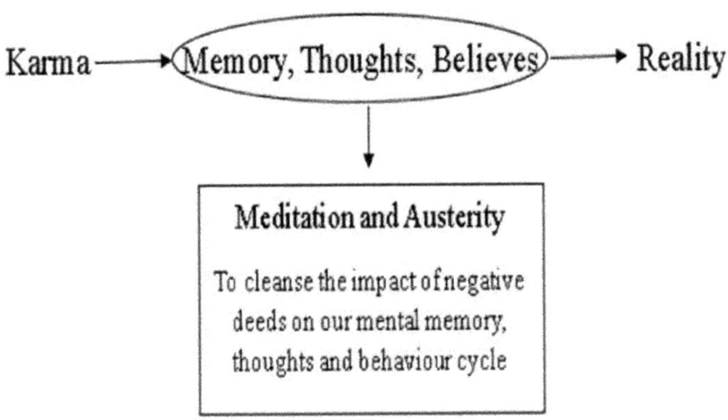
Karma
Memory, Thoughts, Believes
Reality
Meditation and Austerity
To cleanse the impact of negative
deeds on our mental memory,
thoughts and behaviour cycle

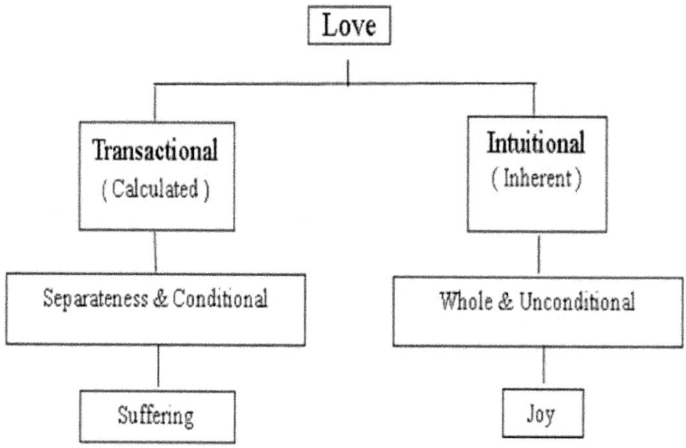
Love
Transactional
(Calculated)
Intuitional
(Inherent)
Separateness & Conditional
Whole & Unconditional
Suffering
Joy

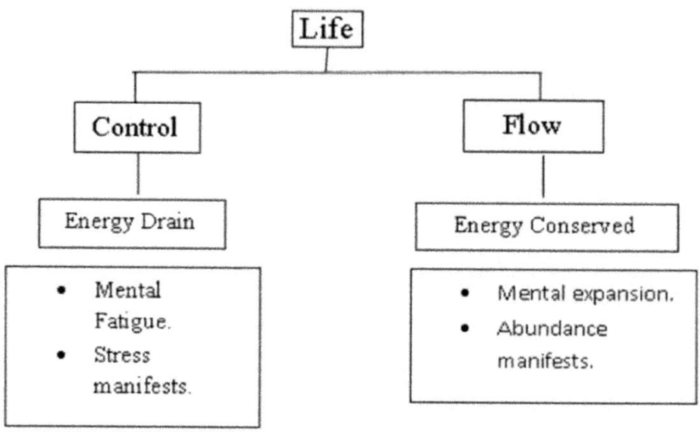
Life
Control
Flow
Energy Drain
Energy Conserved
Mental Fatigue.
Stress manifests.
Mental expansion.
Abundance manifests.

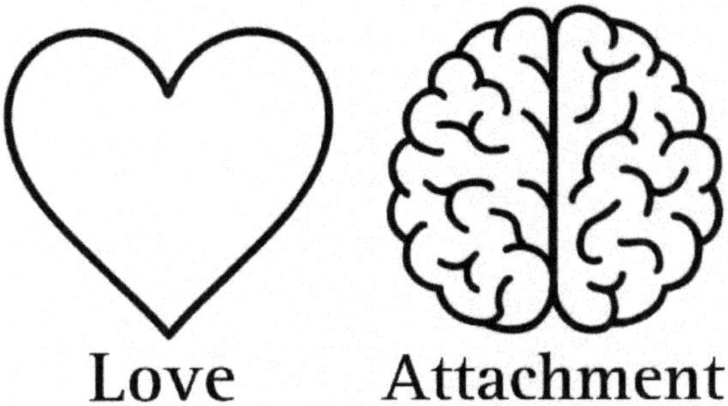
Love
Attachment

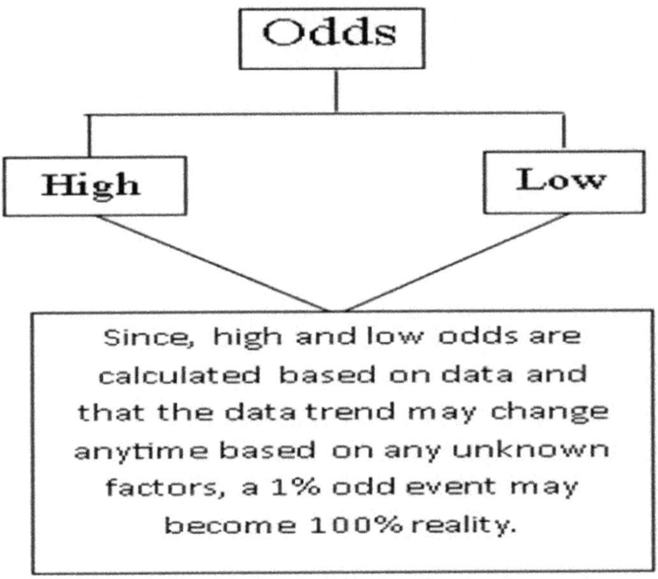
Odds
High
Low
Since, high and low odds are calculated based on data and that the data trend may change anytime based on any unknown factors, a 1% odd event may become 100% reality.

"The woods are lovely, dark and deep,
But I have promises to keep,
And miles to go before I sleep,
And miles to go before I sleep."

-Robert Frost

A POEM TO END…

FAITH'S LULLABY

Lamenting? Oh! You poor soul
This is the hour of grief
Lament, as much thou can,
will it make the hour brief?
Or get intoxicated with a deep sniff
Yes, you are the victim
and the bully is tough and stiff

Hymns and prayers
were not answered
Spirituality is not real
as you only had failure
Faith is a fool's play, hear
Need momentary pleasure,
Precise and clear

Reckon, what did you pray for, dear?
Material pleasures from some unknown seer
Ever asked for energy, divine and sheer?
Remember, Krishna didn't fight
but was the charioteer
Guidance of whose, Arjuna adhered
Mundane journey of yours, let him steer

There are so many with distress and grief
Praying daily to Almighty for relief
So, can you be the answer they receive
For God acts through those who believe
Volunteer for Him and He will never deceive

Say your mind,
Nothing in the world has
the potential to upset you
For you are the part of Him and
He is the part of you
Roaming in this world with some karma due
So why to worry about the worldly fruit,
Seek to be next in His abode's queue

And let this faith guide you
And let this faith guide you

-Sanyam Singhi

CONNECT

Dear Readers,

Writing as an art requires as much mental effort and time from the audience as from the author and since, we have come to the end of this book, I would like to express my deepest gratitude to you for being a part of my journey and enabling me to share my collective experience and perspective on the journey called life.

I would love to connect with you all and hear your perspectives, opinions and feedback regarding the various facets of life and reality shared in this book and things that can be improved.

Instagram- sanyam_singhi

Much Love,
Sanyam

ACKNOWLEDGEMENTS

I extend my deepest thanks to my parents and everyone who has been a part of my life, especially, during the last few years in which I was exposed to myriads of new experiences that have shaped me into the person I am now. To my readers as well, without whose engagement no book can ever serve its purpose and lastly, to everyone who are engaged in the publishing and supply of this book.

www.ingramcontent.com/pod-product-compliance
Ingram Content Group UK Ltd.
Pitfield, Milton Keynes, MK11 3LW, UK
UKHW021400190726
13845UKWH00028B/788

9 789334 391329